MILTON THE MONSTER:
HORROR HILL
EPITAPH

By

Kevin Scott Collier

MILTON THE MONSTER:
HORROR HILL
EPITAPH

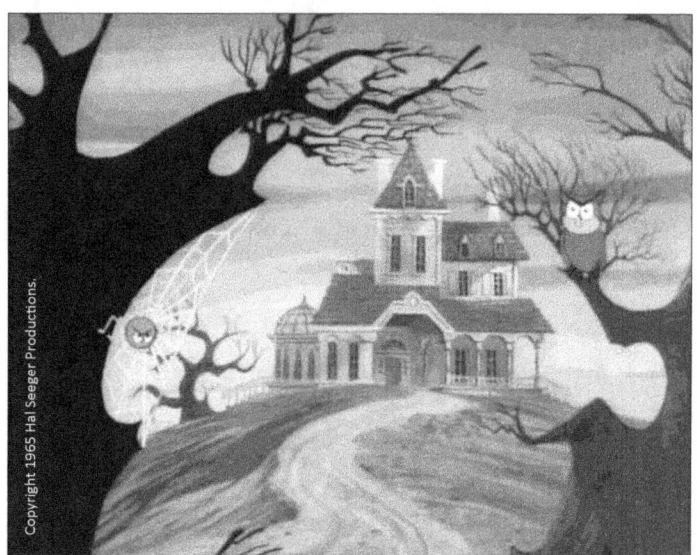

Copyright 1965 Hal Seeger Productions.

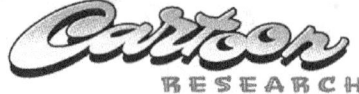

827 North Hollywood Way #100
Burbank, California 91505
Visit us online: www.cartoonresearch.com
Founder: Jerry Beck
Email: jerrybeck18@gmail.com

THIS BOOK IS DEDICATED TO HAL SEEGER.

A special thanks to Jerry Beck, who provided original documents and artwork from the "The Milton the Monster Show,"
and to Jim Engel for providing his VHS cover artwork for Siren
Entertainment's 1999 video releases.

MILTON THE MONSTER: HORROR HILL EPITAPH is written and compiled by Kevin Scott Collier.
Sources: Jerry Beck, the cartoon series itself, entertainment periodicals, promotional documents
from the series, Library of Congress archives and misc. animation resources and historical sites.

They Came from Horror Hill

"The Milton the Monster Show" was my earliest favorite cartoon. I was only the age of 8 when Milton brought Horror Hill onto the small screen. I liked him so much, I learned to draw him, and drew many illustrations of the gentle creature for my classmates at school.

The most attractive aspect of Milton and his co-stars was that they were monsters. What kid doesn't like monsters? But adding to the attraction was the fact that this show didn't scare you. Monsters are cool, but at age 8, you don't need to go to bed at night wondering if there's something hiding beneath your mattress.

My parents even liked Milton. Now I can see the humor and satire written into the series that only adults would understand. All of it entirely appropriate for younger viewers, of course. But Milton was also from an age before Political Correctness, and today sometimes draws attention to a time when environments were less civil and fair.

Living with Milton in the castle atop Horror Hill was his creator, Professor Weirdo, a short man with a commanding voice. His assistant and partner in mischief is Count Kook.

Milton's siblings, if you can call them that, are Heebie and Jeebie. Heebie is a skeleton-like character who possesses a voice akin to actor Peter Lorre. Jeebie is a light-green furry creature, sporting a single fang and having one eye. The ghoulish pair can sometimes be part of the problem for Professor Weirdo, instead of a solution.

Milton is the problem. Adding a little too much tenderness potion, the monster became a polite, loving, gentle giant, with a voice akin to actor Jim Nabors' Gomer Pyle persona.

Living nearby is Professor Weirdo's nemesis, Professor Fruitcake. He's created a pair of zombies, Abercrombie and Zelda, who live with him. Partnering with Fruitcake, on occasion to present opposition to Professor Weirdo, is Fangenstein. Fangy rides a supped-up motorcycle, and dresses like he's in a cycle gang.

None of them possess much in the way of intel-

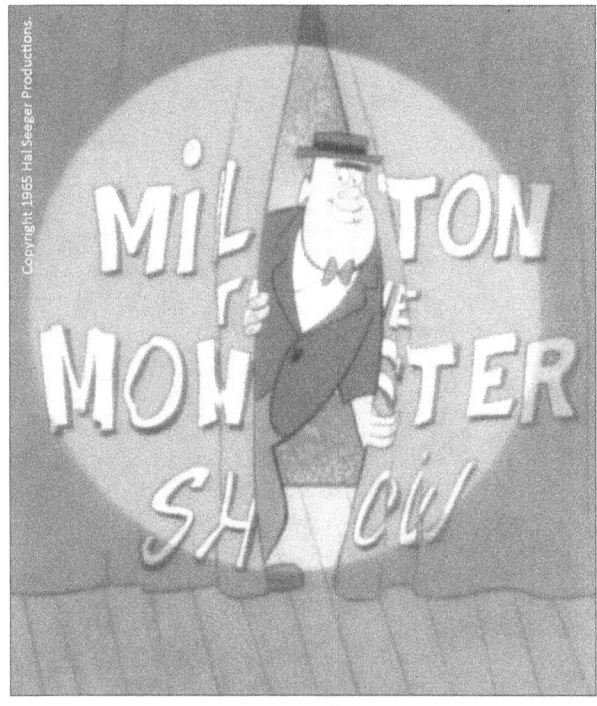

Milton the Monster stepped onto the stage October 9, 1965, on ABC Television Network. *Copyright 1965 Hal Seeger Productions.*

ligence. "The Milton the Monster Show" was more about acting on rumor, or impulse, rather than fact. And loyalty only went as far as the next disagreement between any members. They were lovable characters, but you couldn't trust them. Well, only one. Milton.

I wasn't the greatest fan of the show's backup characters, such as Penny Penguin and Flukey Luke. Stuffy Durma was fun, in a "Beverly Hillbillies," rags-to-riches kind of way.

The main accompanying cartoon in the show was Fearless Fly, who originally was the intended Hal Seeger Productions project. "The Milton the Monster Show" originally began production as "The Fearless Fly Show."

Fearless Fly is a super-powered insect whose opponents, Dr. Goo Fee and Gung Ho, keep him quite busy. The character was a big hit with fans of the show.

Enjoy the book, and don't be frightened!

Kevin Scott Collier

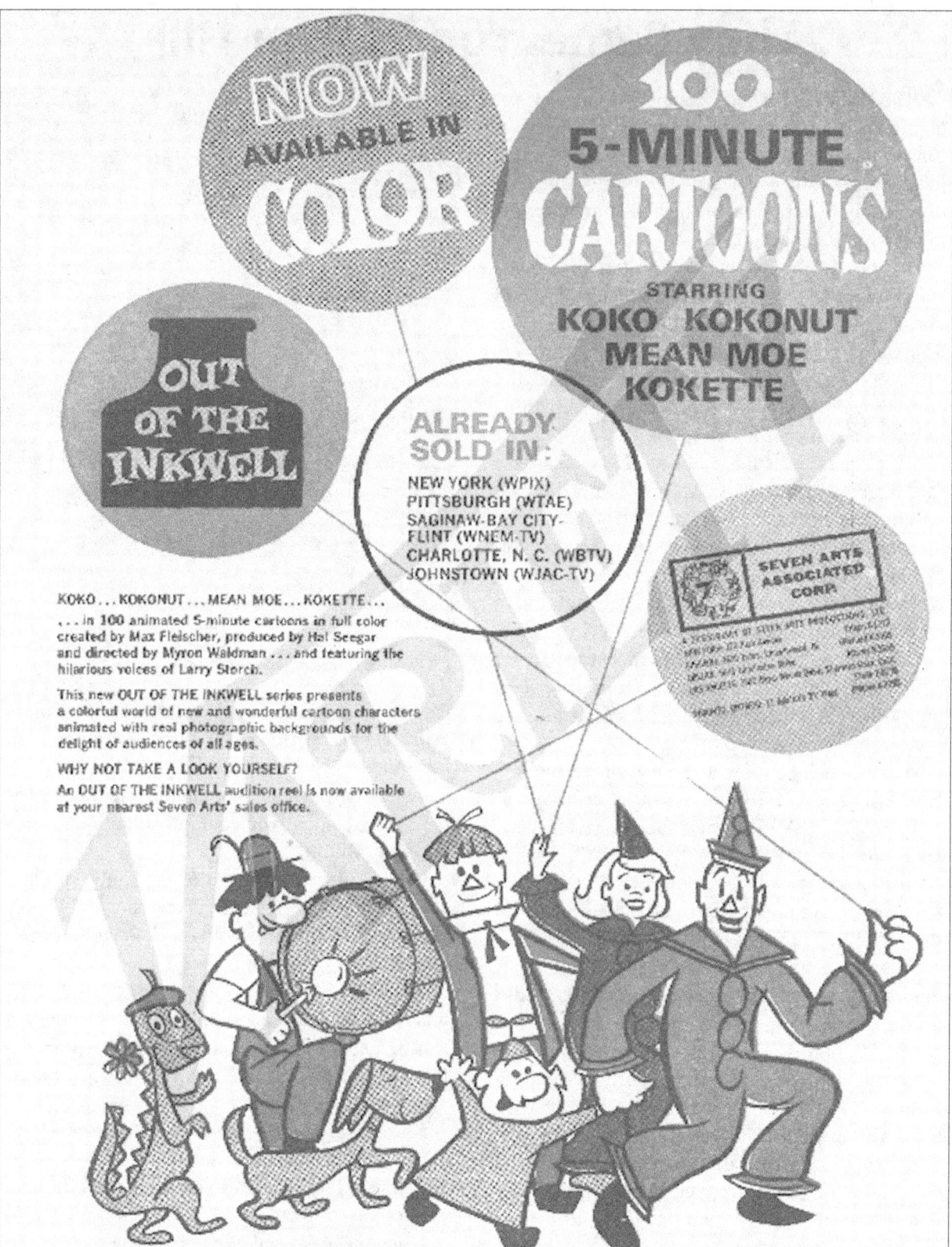

The Road to Hal Seeger Productions

"The Milton the Monster Show" creator, Hal Seeger, departed this world on March 13, 2005, at the age of 87. However, his gentle monstrous creation lives on.

Created in the fictitious laboratory, by his inventor-father, Professor Weirdo, Milton the Monster first appeared on the ABC Television Network on October 9, 1965, and ended rerun status on September 8, 1968. The program presented 78 cartoons in all, three per show, compiled within 26, 30-minute episodes.

Besides Professor Weirdo, Milton's escapades also included regular characters Count Kook, Heebie and Jeebie. Supporting characters included Professor Fruitcake, Abercrombie and Zelda the Zombies, Fangenstein, and others.

Additional cartoons in "The Milton the Monster Show" featured characters such as Flukey Luke, Muggy-Doo, and Fearless Fly.

In fact, Fearless Fly was initially the designated star of the planned animated television series, until Milton popped up in pre-production.

Harold "Hal" Seeger's life began in Brooklyn, New York, on May 16, 1917. According to Seeger, he started out as "a kid cartoonist," finding his first trade job of merit with Max Fleischer at the age of 17, as an opaquer.

Seeger next landed a professional stint as a continuity writer for cartoonist Bud Counihan, who was doing the "Betty Boop" comic strip. Seeger was delighted with the spot.

Dave Fleischer offered Seeger a position as a cartoon writer, and he accepted, with the conclusion of the Betty Boop comic strip. The arrangement included scripting "Paramount News" promotional pieces for Popeye, Betty Boop and other characters.

Upon a studio move to Florida, Seeger was offered an opportunity to produce a slide-show project for the anti-defamation league B'nai B'rith. Seeger suggested it be a six-minute animated cartoon, and came up with an idea to offset the cost of the project, by soliciting donations and having

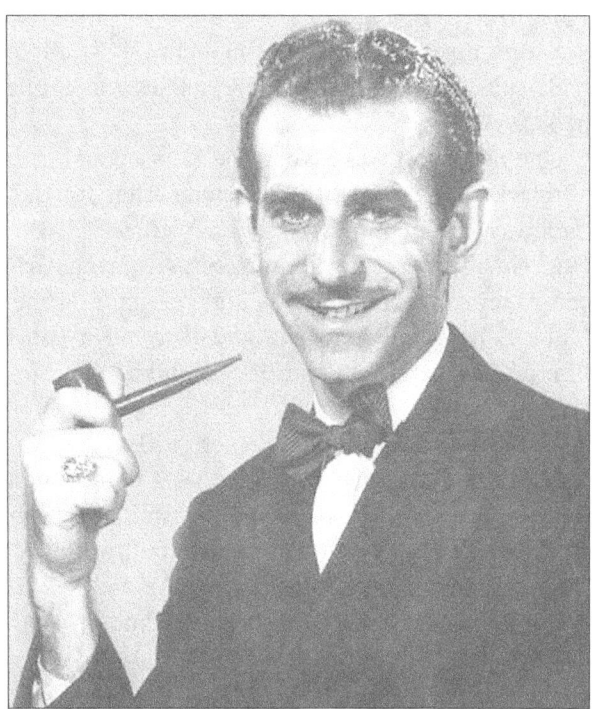
Harold "Hal" Seeger, founder of Hal Seeger Productions.

professionals volunteer their time and skills. Seeger contacted Paramount president, Barney Balaban, encouraging him to write a letter to Max Fleischer requesting the use of his facilities. Max Fleischer agreed to the arrangement, with Seeger driving the project after office hours at 5:00 p.m.

With the cooperation of co-workers and donations, Seeger pulled off the project for only $215.

When the United States entered World War II, Seeger was sent straight to Washington, D.C. (Due to a bum leg, Seeger didn't serve overseas or see combat). A meeting with Lieutenant Herb Bradford, on the base, encouraged Seeger on his pathway of writing, producing and directing military films.

In an interview recalling the events, conducted by Jerry Beck, and published in the November 1980 issue of "Mindrot," Seeger spoke of the experience.

"They gave me a job as senior motion picture writer. I couldn't type. I couldn't spell," Seeger said. "But I sat down and wrote training films throughout the war. When I left the army, I continued with the writing, not with the animation at all. I just wrote."

Seeger made his living writing many short, three reel, subject films and writing stories for comic books.

One film short was a Keystone Kops spoof "with all black cops." Seeger was a screenwriter for Cab Calloway's 1947 musical motion picture "Hi-De-Ho." He also wrote for film projects featuring African-American actors Dusty Fletcher and Moms Mabley. By 1950, he wrote and directed a short film for Warner Brothers titled "Hands Tell a Story."

In the world of comics, Seeger worked for National Periodicals, which became DC Comics, then other comics book publishers, as well. He spun stories for "A Date with Judy," "Leave it to Binky," "Henry Aldrich" and other funny books.

Comic books appealed to Seeger. Thus, in 1953

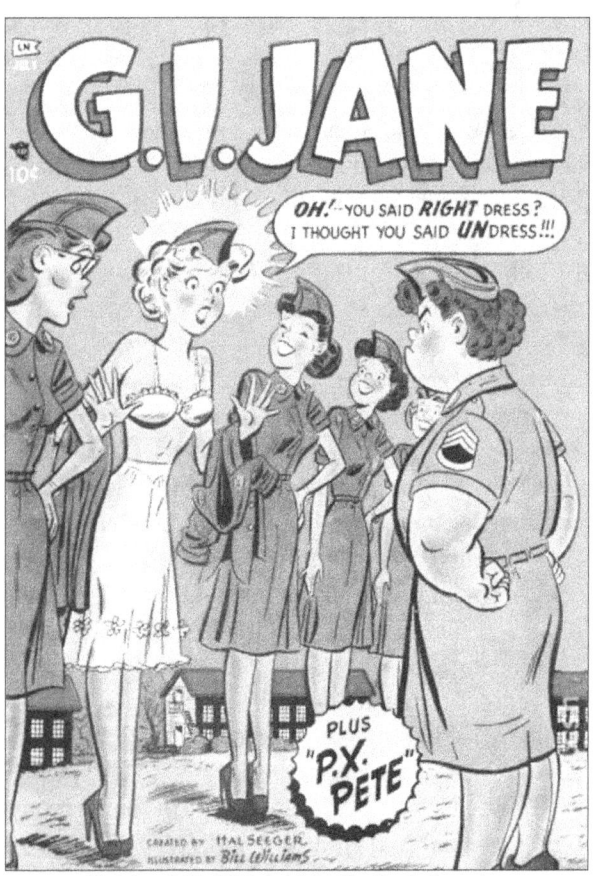

"G. I. Jane" #8, 1953, published by Stanhall comics.

he co-founded a publishing company, with partner Stanley Estrow, named Stanhall. Bill Williams was the chief artist for the business. The venture published six humorous titles, featuring characters like G. I. Jane, a female version of G. I. Joe, and Muggy-Doo, a boy cat. The company, located on Lexington Avenue in Manhattan, went out of business shortly after it changed its name to Merit Publishing, in 1955.

"But we failed," Seeger said. "We couldn't compete with the big guys. I decided to give up the comic book business and go back into the animation business."

In the late 1950's Seeger founded Hal Seeger Productions, in New York. After a brief period operating from a hotel, the business opened its doors at 200 West 54th Street. A steady flow of work came from product manufacturers that desired, or required, animation in their TV commercials.

"I would take a job and tell them how to do it," Seeger told "Mindrot" magazine. "I'd go out and freelance it around. I'd go to different animators, like Al Stahl, who was in the business, and I would have these guys do the animation."

Hal Seeger Productions moved to 48 West, 48th Street next, and was equipped with all the bells and whistles to engage in full in-house animation work. One early success was creating the animated Campbell soup kids.

"Then I started doing 'Out of the Inkwell' with Max Fleischer," Seeger noted. "I did a hundred 'Out of the Inkwell' [shorts]."

Seeger's "Out of the Inkwell" series brought back many classic Fleischer characters and featured the voice of actor Larry Storch.

Animator Myron Waldman remembered, in a 1994 interview, Hal Seeger's desire to resurrected Fleischer's Inkwell.

"I did a layout for the pilot episode so he could get backers," Waldman said. "One of the changes we made in the series was that I updated Koko's look and since we couldn't use Betty Boop and others, we created new characters like the female Koketee and Koko-nut, his dog."

During the growth into a formidable animation

studio, Seeger brought in many talented individuals that became synonymous with his production company.

"I hired all of the people who ever worked for me," Seeger said. "Myron Waldman, Shamus Culhane, top cartoonist, Orestes Calpini, George Rufle, one of the old-timers. Tommy Golden, Marty Taras, Dave Tendlar. I mean, all the top guys. They all worked on 'Out of the Inkwell.'"

There was one person on the payroll Seeger didn't hire. It was voice artist Beverly Arnold. Seeger had married her.

In 1964, Hal Seeger Productions took over animating the opening and closing sequences of Warner Brothers' "The Porky Pig Show."

Following "The Milton the Monster Show," Hal Seeger Productions released another animated series, "Batfink," which first appeared on television the spring of 1966.

"Before 'Batman' [the Adam West live-action series] was making it big on television, before it even hit the air, I did 'Batfink,'" Seeger said.

The series included 100 short cartoons, featuring costumed superhero bat, Batfink, his assistant, Karate, and a colorful variety of bad guys.

While "The Milton the Monster Show" and "Batfink" became classics in the TV animation world, producing animated series proved to be too much effort and a financial risk.

"After I was done with 'Batfink,' I lost like $125,000-$130,000. So, I said, 'That's the end of my series, that's the last one I'm doing.'"

Seeger eventually made his financial losses back

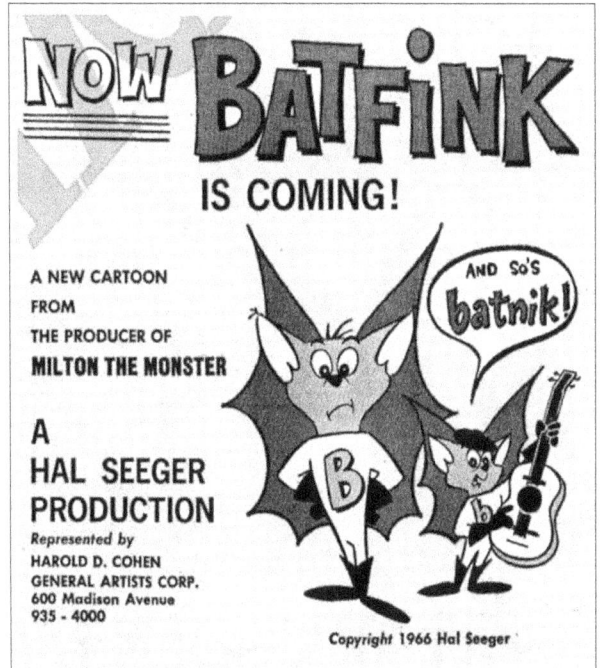

Ad for "Batfink," 1966. *Copyright 1966 Hal Seeger Productions.*

in time, many times over, but dropped out of the cartoon grind.

"It was too much of a rat race. I never wanted to do it again; it was too big for me," Seeger said.

Hal Seeger Productions continued in business for decades, providing an array of services for the film industry and the growing video imaging market. Several millions of dollars went into upgrading the studios to keep up with demands.

His brief legacy producing cartoons for television cemented his place in animation history.

Hal Seeger made his residence at Great Neck, New York, at the time of his death in 2005.

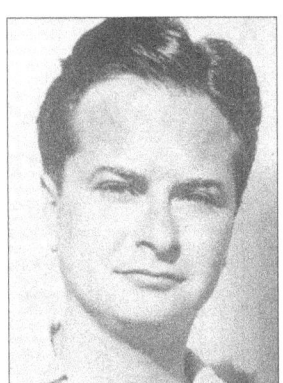
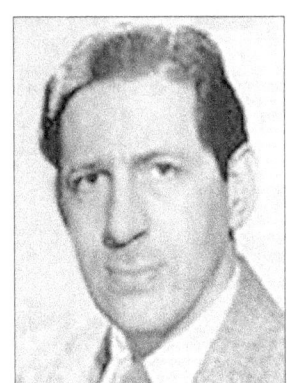
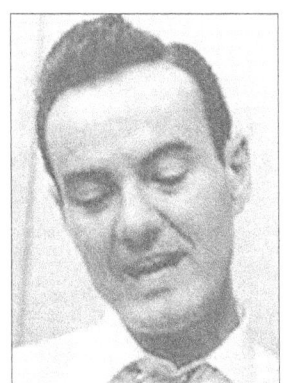
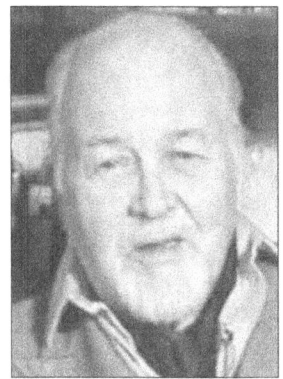

Left to right, part of the Hal Seeger Productions team: Myron Waldman, Dayton Allen, Bob McFadden and Shamus Culhane.

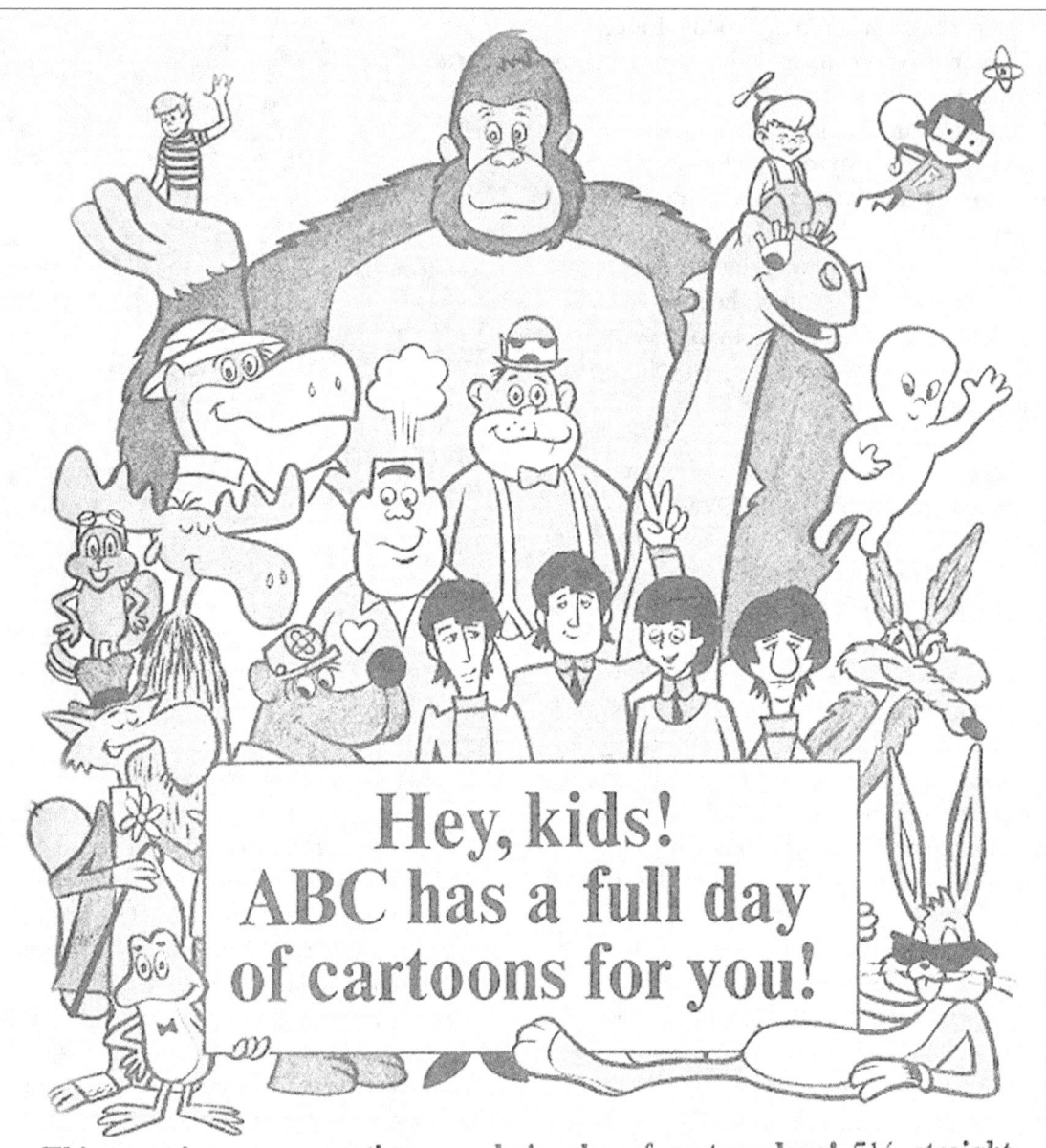

Hey, kids!
ABC has a full day
of cartoons for you!

This morning, see a continuous who's who of cartoondom! 5½ straight hours of your favorite comic heroes, all in color! King Kong, The Beatles, new Casper the Ghost cartoons, Bugs Bunny, Milton the Monster, Fearless Fly, Beany and Cecil, Magilla Gorilla, Peter Potamus, Bullwinkle and Hoppity Hooper. All this topped off by the great teen music show, Where the Action Is. For a day-after-turkey-day treat, join ABC's Holiday Cartoon Jubilee!

abc In Color, Starting at 10:00 am 6 9 10

ABC Television Network advertisement for their cartoon new line-up, which included "The Milton the Monster Show." Fearless Fly appears at top, right. *Copyright 1965 Hal Seeger Productions.*

The Genesis of Milton the Monster

The genesis of Milton the Monster, and the show bearing him name, transpired during Hal Seeger's production of "The Fearless Fly Show."

Seeger had completed three Fearless Fly adventures, presenting Professor Weirdo and Count Kook, who lived in a haunted mansion atop Horror Hill, as the hero's opponents. The first story, "Fly by Might," introduced a gentle fly, named Hiram, who, upon wearing special spectacles, became Fearless Fly. The tiny hero was said to derive his superpowers from the pair of glasses, which generated millions of megatons of energy through the sensitive muscles in his head.

The first adventure also introduced Hiram's friends, Flory, a sexy female fly he is sweet on, and a lovable bully named Horsey, a horsefly. While Hiram/Fearless Fly lived in a matchbox, the trio gathered inside a sugar bowl, which served as a recreational venue and hangout.

The first adventure also featured a different narrator that delivered his lines in a tone indicative of mystery dramas.

In "Fly by Might," Professor Weirdo is first depicted driving an early horseless, carriage-type, automobile in the city, looking for animals he can supersize with his atom enlarger device to cause havoc.

Weirdo lives in an old house atop Horror Hill, which is said to be his laboratory. His appearance and voice are identical to the character appearing in Milton the Monster adventures. However, Weirdo's attire is purple, not red, as in the Milton series. Professor Weirdo is alone.

The episode was animated by Myron Walden.

The second Fearless Fly adventure produced, "The Spider Spiter," added another character to what would become the Milton the Monster cast. It introduced Count Kook. His appearance and voice are identical to the character appearing in Milton the Monster adventures.

This tale depicts Weirdo and Kook in a laboratory, complete with beakers and bubbling potions.

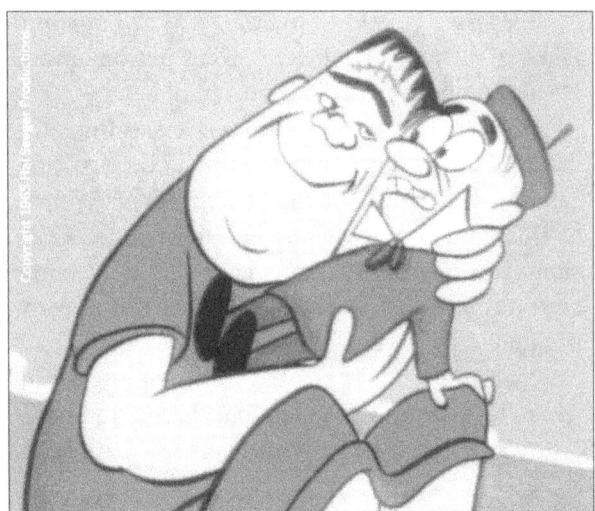

George the Monster with his creator, Professor Weirdo, as he first appeared in the Fearless Fly episode "Fearless Fly Meets the Monsters." *Copyright 1965 Hal Seeger Productions.*

A giant spider also appears, a likeness of which later appears in background scenes in the Milton series.

The episode was animated by Shamus Culhane.

In the third Fearless Fly adventure produced, "Fearless Fly Meets the Monsters," the inspiration for the Milton the Monster character appears, when Professor Weirdo cooks up a Frankenstein-like monster named George. Milton's strange siblings, Heebie and Jeebie, are also depicted, as well as and a mechanical man. All went unnamed, in what some animation historians call the "Milton pilot" episode.

The laboratory scene in which the monster is created was recreated as the opening of each Milton cartoon and the dialogue during the scene was rewritten creating "The Milton the Monster Show" theme song.

In "Fearless Fly Meets the Monsters," Count Kook doesn't bump Professor Weirdo's arm, causing him to spill too much of the "tincture of tenderness" potion.

Voice artist, Bob McFadden, delivered a deep, dopey voice for the monster, not the Gomer Pyle style heard in the Milton series. George the Monster also had red stitches on his forehead and displayed a head hair. He also does not blow smoke from the top of his head.

George is brought to town by Count Kook and takes in a monster movie, scaring patrons away. He also scares a girl seated on a park bench.

Fearless Fly arrives on the scene and finds the creature to be kind and friendly. The two play catch with a ball. Kook informs Professor Weirdo of this, and he dispatches the other three monsters to destroy George. They knock George around, but Fearless knocks all three out of commission.

Fearless Fly takes George to a clothing store, where he's dressed in a plaid purple suit and hat.

It was this adventure that plans for "The Fear-less Fly Show" took a turn in a different direction.

Bob McFadden recalled the genesis of Milton the Monster and the transition from a show named after Fearless Fly to the gentle giant, in "The Magic Behind the Voices," written by Tim Lawson and Alisa Parsons, published in 2004.

"On the third show of that series, Fearless Fly goes into a place and meets a benign monster called Milton," McFadden said. "The producers, the animators, and everyone flipped over the character. No one in the public had seen it yet, but everybody was so crazy about the character and what was happening with it that they decided to change the name of the show from 'Fearless Fly' to 'Milton the Monster' with Fearless Fly segments."

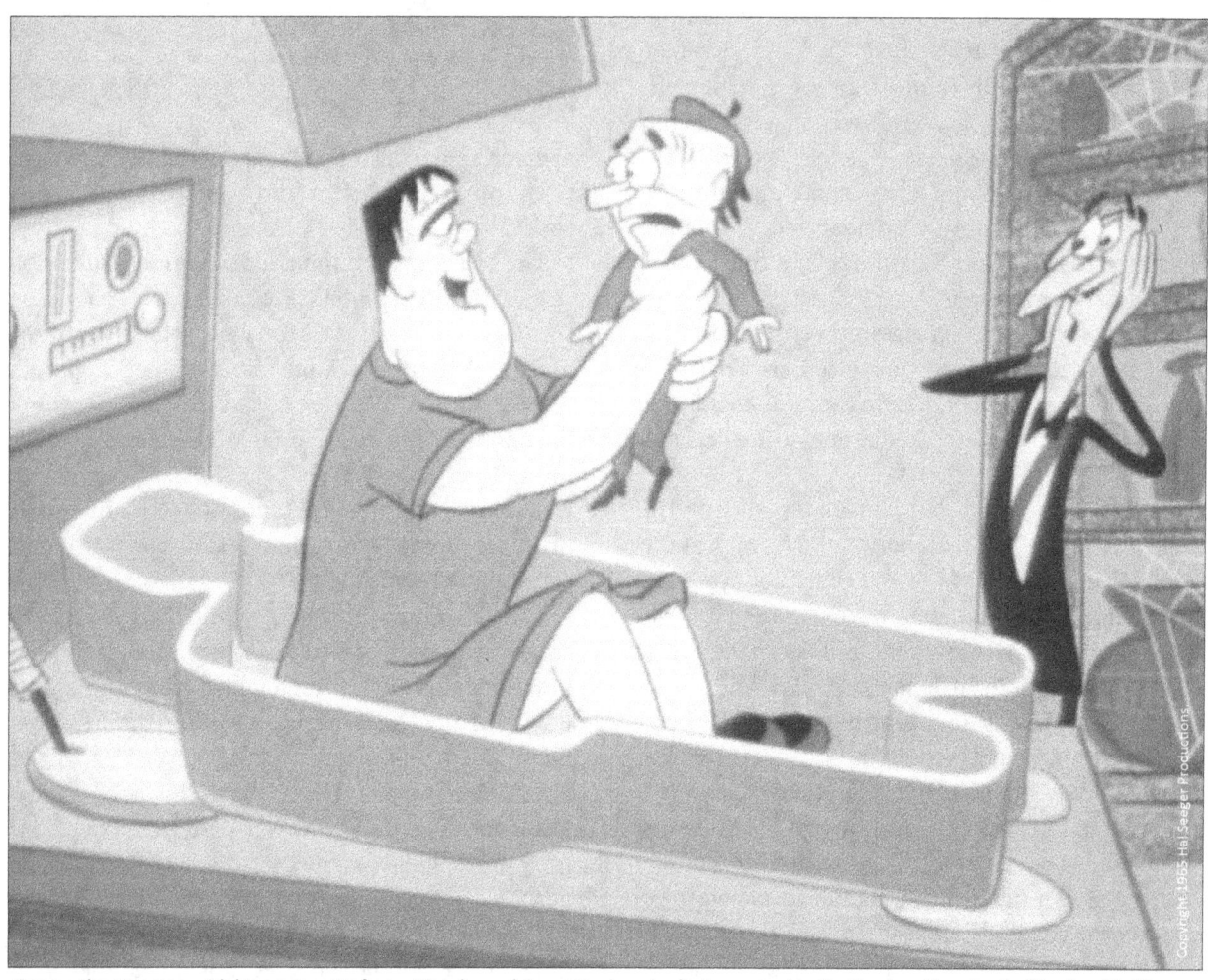

George the Monster, with his creator, Professor Weirdo, and Count Kook, as he first appeared in the Fearless Fly episode "Fearless Fly Meets the Monsters." *Copyright 1965 Hal Seeger Productions.*

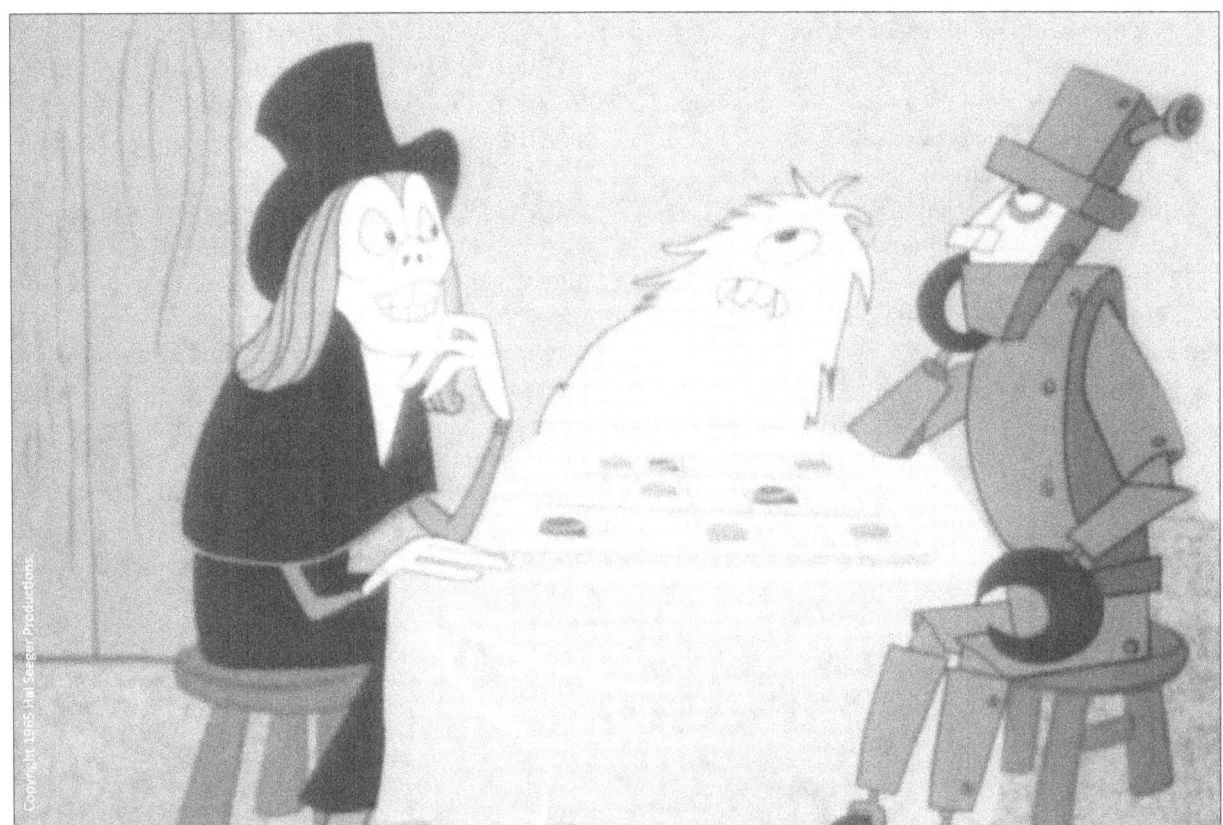

Heebie, left and Jeebie, middle, as they first appeared in the Fearless Fly episode "Fearless Fly Meets the Monsters." A mechanical man was also presented as a creation of Weirdo in the story. *Copyright 1965 Hal Seeger Productions.*

George the Monster was renamed and redesigned for his own series. Animator Shamus Culhane came up with the name Milton, which had a ring to it. So, Milton the Monster it was. Hal Seeger knew he had a winner with the modified series and pitched it for television.

"I sold the series to ABC Network," Seeger said in "Mindrot" magazine #19, published November 1980. Conducting the interview was Jerry Beck, presently an animation historian, author, and founder of Cartoon Research.

"Milton the Monster, with Fearless Fly. Shamus [Culhane], Myron [Waldman]. Then I started hiring real writers, and we did a heck of a job on 'Milton the Monster,'" Seeger said.

Shamus Culhane and Myron Waldman were two of the more than two dozen talented individuals at Hal Seeger Productions who were involved in the program's production.

Unlike his predecessor, George, Milton the Monster was given a more friendly appearance. Heebie and Jeebie were given makeover, too. Heebie became more skeleton-like and Jeebie was given a single fang as a tooth. The mechanical man, or robot, was dropped altogether.

Another change made after "Fearless Fly Meets the Monsters," involved a voice switch. Heebie became the voice of Jeebie, and Jeebie became the voice of Heebie.

Now that Milton was to star in his own series, discussion concerning Professor Weirdo, Count Kook surfaced. Both could no longer be opponents of Fearless Fly. Thus Dr. Goo Fee, a 973-year-old wizard and his dunce assistant named Gung Ho were invented for that series.

A decision was made that the opening for Milton the Monster adventures should depict his origin. Lyrics for the theme song were based on dialogue from George the Monster's creation in "Fearless Fly Meets the Monsters."

"Six drops of the essence of terror,
Five drops of sinister sauce,
When the stirring's done may I lick the spoon?
Of course, ha ha, of course.
Now for the tincture of tenderness,
But I must use only a touch,
For without a touch of tenderness,
He might destroy me!

(Professor Weirdo, bumped) Whoops, too much.

(Weirdo) Better hold your breath it's starting to tick:

(Count Kook) Better hold my hand I'm feeling sick -

(Milton) Hello, Dad!

(Weirdo) What have I done?

(Milton) I'm Milton, your brand new son!"

There was no intention, due to the investment, to scrap the completed first three Fearless Fly adventures. Thus, they were included in "The Milton the Monster Show."

To avoid confusion with viewers regarding who Fearless Fly's arch enemies were—Dr. Goo Fee and Gung Ho—it was decided the three adventures featuring Professor Weirdo be placed midway in the series. Doing so created an impression the trio of Horror Hill episodes were whimsical crossover tales. Also, Weirdo was creating another monster—George—not Milton.

Milton's siblings were given the names Heebie and Jeebie in recognition of the creepy, anxiety-driven term, "He gives me the heebie-jeebies."

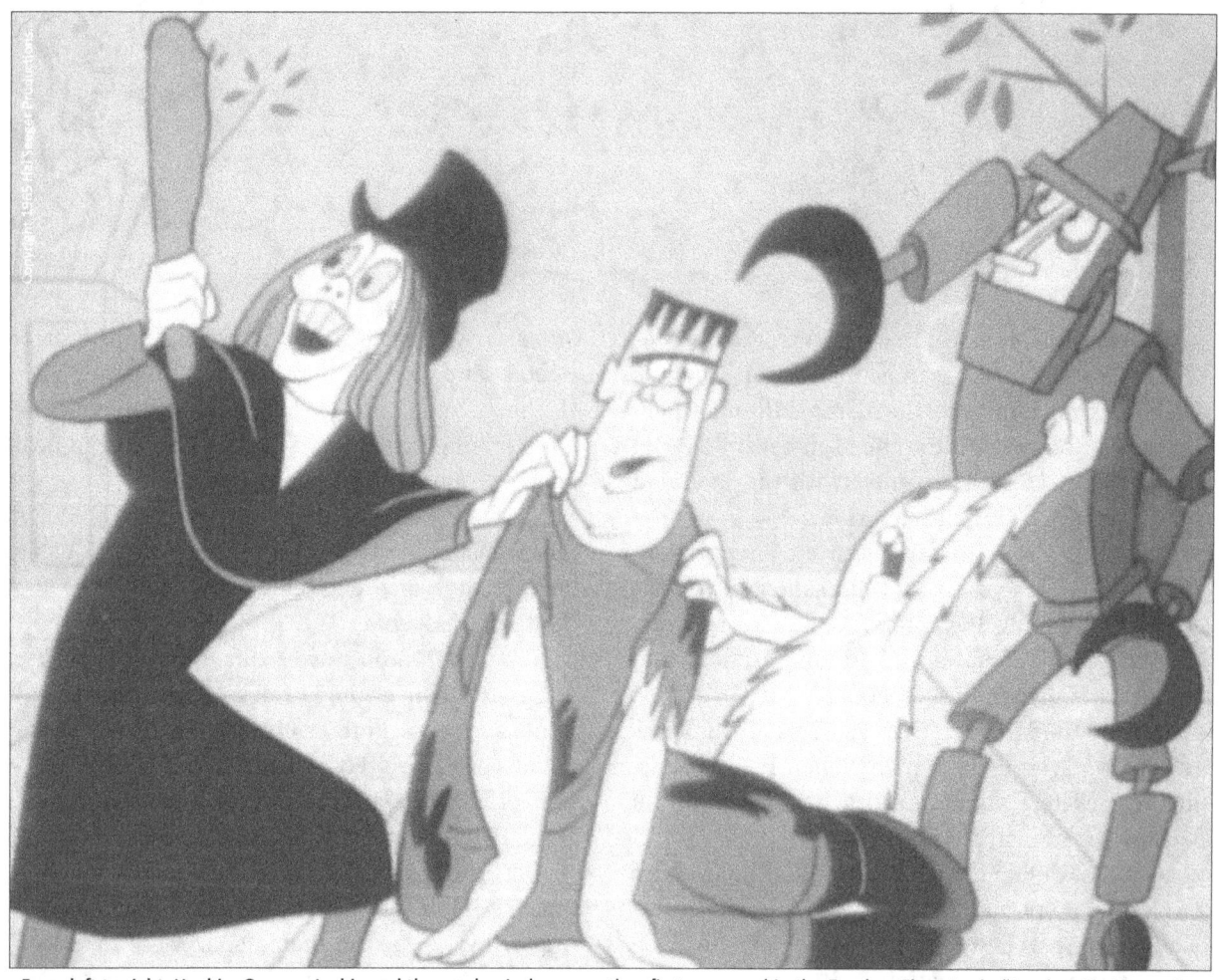

From left to right, Heebie, George, Jeebie and the mechanical man, as they first appeared in the Fearless Fly episode "Fearless Fly Meets the Monsters." *Copyright 1965 Hal Seeger Productions.*

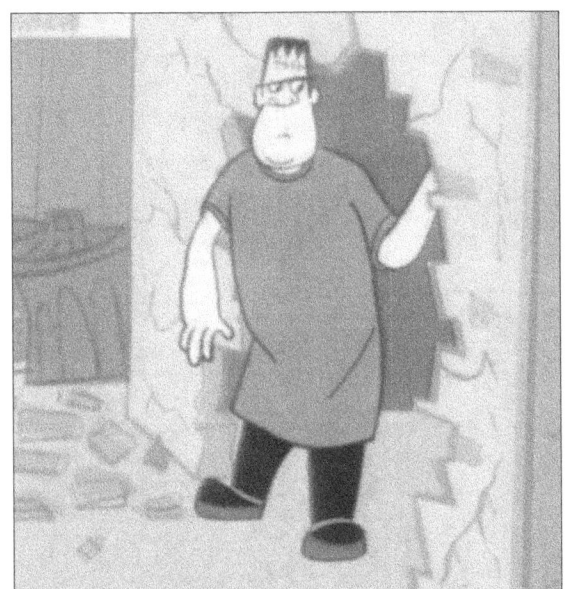
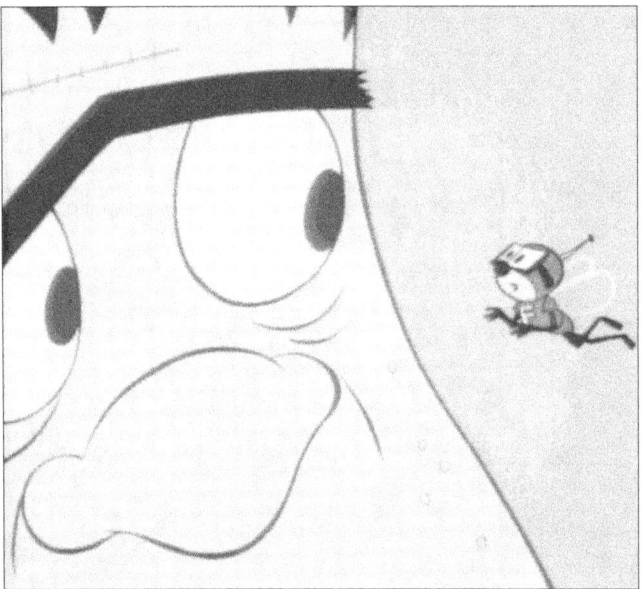

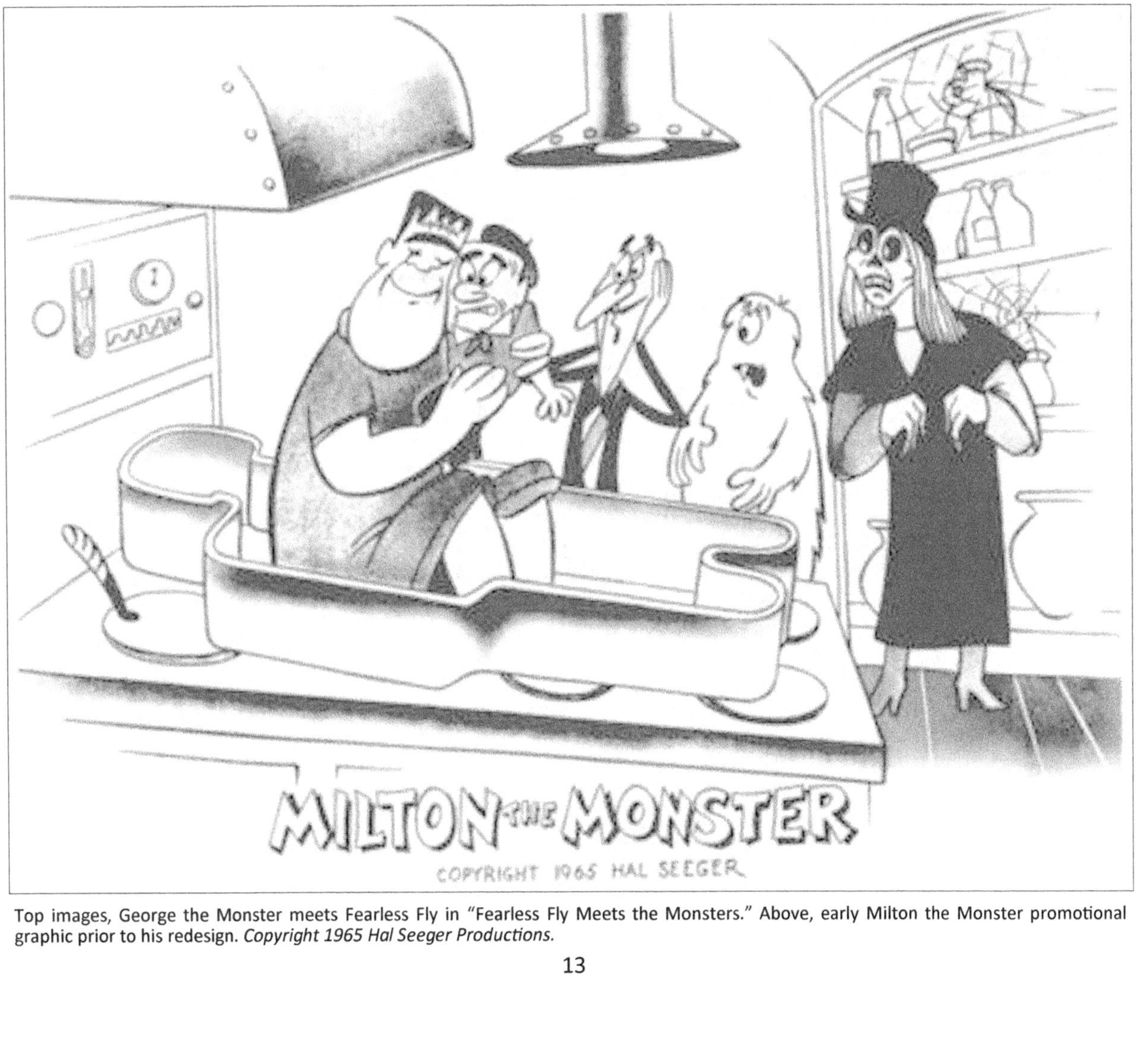

Top images, George the Monster meets Fearless Fly in "Fearless Fly Meets the Monsters." Above, early Milton the Monster promotional graphic prior to his redesign. *Copyright 1965 Hal Seeger Productions.*

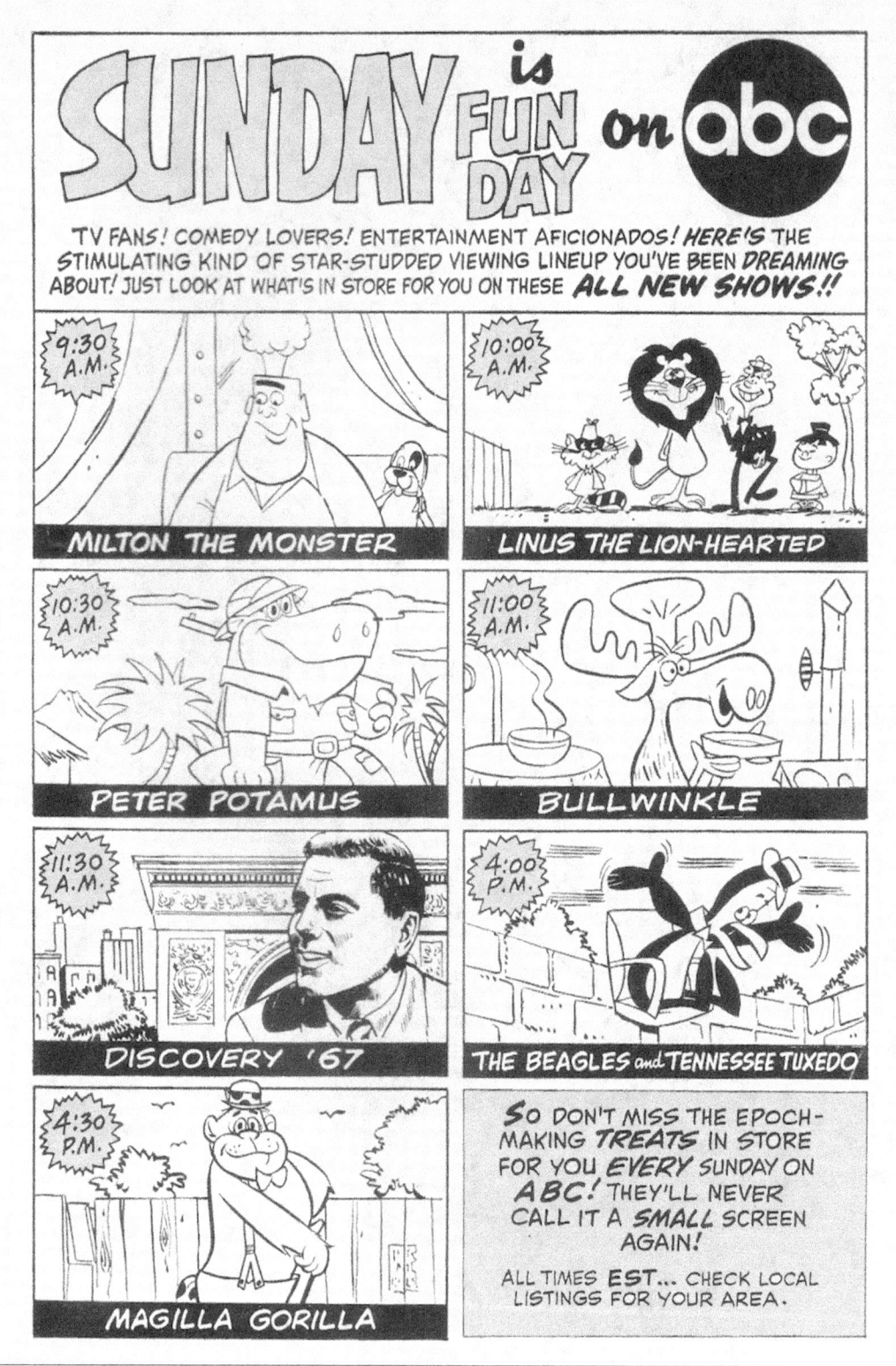

ABC Television Network advertisement for their cartoon new line-up, which included "The Milton the Monster Show." *Copyright 1965 Hal Seeger Productions.*

14

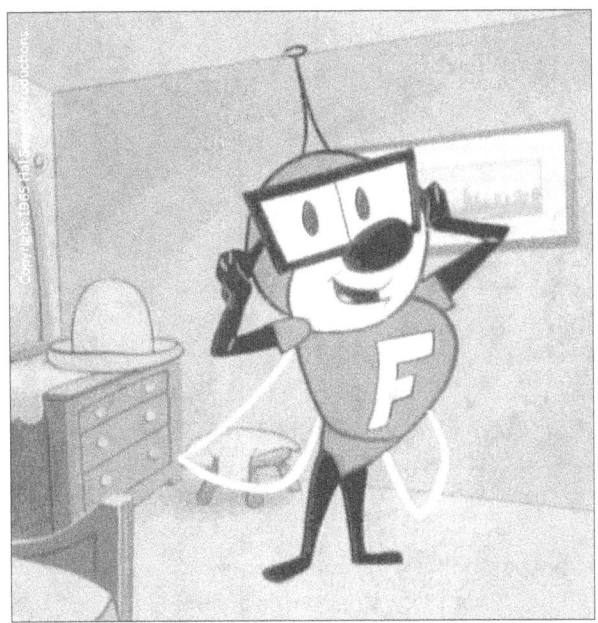

Hiram Fly changes into Fearless Fly. *Copyright 1965 Hal Seeger Productions.*

Joining Milton and Fearless in "The Milton the Monster Show" were revolving cartoon titles "Muggy-Doo," "Flukey Luke," "Stuffy Durma" and "Penny Penguin."

The character Muggy-Doo, a boy fox, wasn't above breaking the law and deceiving others to get what he wanted, and that usually involved money. Hal Seeger borrowed the name from a character he'd created, first published in Stanhall Comics in 1953, "Muggy-Doo the Boy Cat." The comic book series, written by Seeger, was illustrated by Irving Spector. Seeger also made an animated pilot for a series about the character, but it proved to be too expensive to produce and wasn't to his liking. He sold it to Paramount as a single cartoon and they exhibited it theatrically in 1963.

"When I did Milton, I changed the name to Muggy-Doo, boy fox," Seeger said in "Mindrot" magazine. "I made a few of them [cartoons], but it didn't make it for me. So, I didn't keep it."

The character Stuffy Durma, a hobo who inherited ten million dollars, lived in a townhouse with his assistant and secretary, Bradley Brinkley, and a staff of servants. Seeger had borrowed the name from his "Stuffy Derma" character, a secondary series in the back pages of the "Muggy-Doo the

Other supporting characters in the Milton series included Professor Weirdo's nasty nemesis Professor Fruitcake, and his creatures, Zelda and Abercrombie the Zombies. A biker version of Frankenstein, known as Fangenstein, riding a motorcycle armed with an arsenal of weaponry, often worked with Fruitcake.

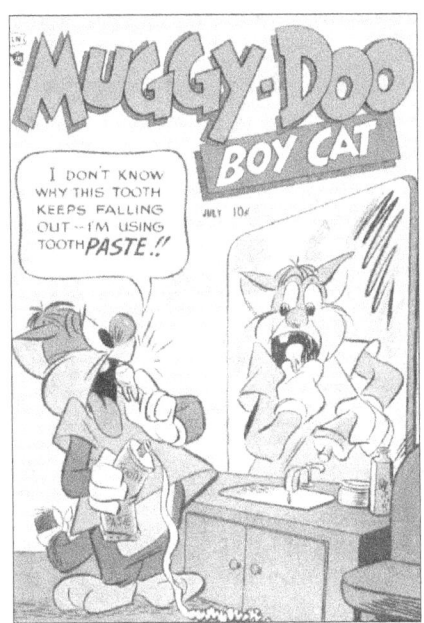

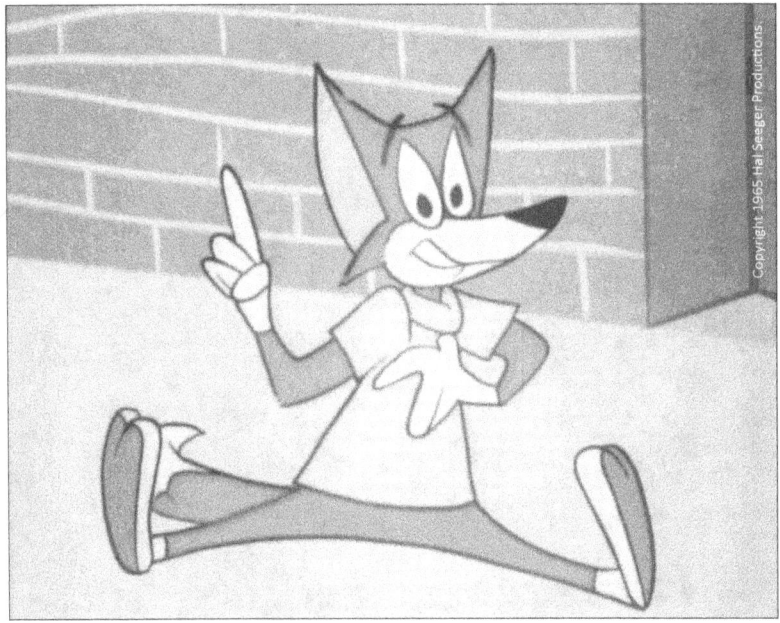

Right, Muggy-Doo, originally was a boy cat in a 1953 comic book series. Left, Muggy-Doo, boy fox, as he appeared in "The Milton the Monster Show." *Copyright 1965 Hal Seeger Productions.*

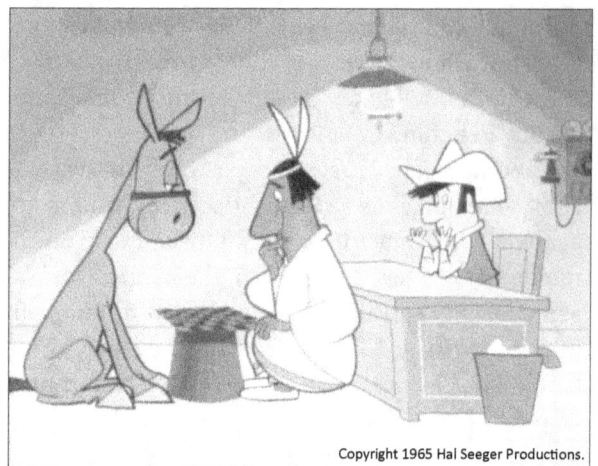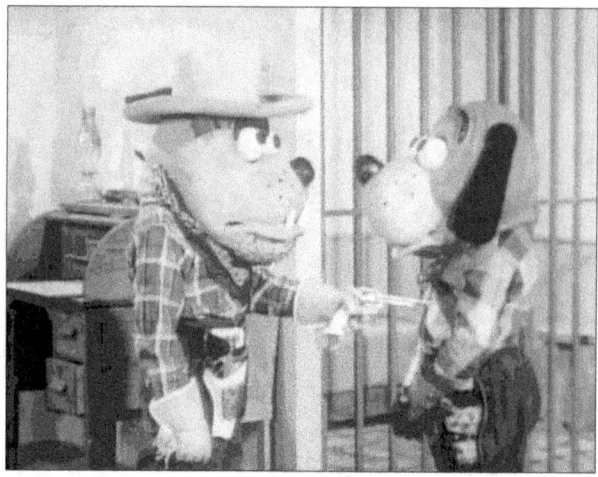

Copyright 1965 Hal Seeger Productions.

Left, Pronto the horse, Two Feathers, a Native-American, and Flukey Luke as they appeared in "The Milton the Monster Show." At right, Flukey Luke, the dog without hat, as he appeared in the live-action pilot. *Copyright 1965 Hal Seeger Productions.*

Boy Cat" comic book. The character originally was a pig that found himself in precarious situations.

The character Flukey Luke also was a borrowed name, based on a live-action show Seeger filmed a pilot for in the mid-1950's. In the original, Flukey was a dog that was a sheriff. Actors wore costume animal heads and sported human attire. In the cartoon series produced for "The Milton the Monster Show," Flukey Luke was a cowboy in the city who worked as a Private Eye. His companions included a faithful Indian named Two Feathers, and Flukey's horse, Pronto.

The character Penny Penguin, a spoiled brat little girl, routinely caused problems and disaster everywhere she went. In the series, she lives in a suburban home with her parents.

Over two dozen talented individuals juggled the titles packing them into "The Milton the Monster Show."

The Hal Seeger Productions staff included writers Jack Mercer, Heywood King and Seeger. Animators included Myron Waldman, Shamus Culhane, Ray Seti, Izzy Klein, Bill Ackerman, Graham Palace, Otto Feuer, Morey Reden, James Tyer, John Gentilella, Irving Dressler, Tom Golden, Arnie Levey and John Tyer. Background artists included Frank Dorso, Robert Owen, and John Zago.

Voice artists on the show included Bob McFadden, Herb Duncan, Dayton Allen, Hetty Galen,

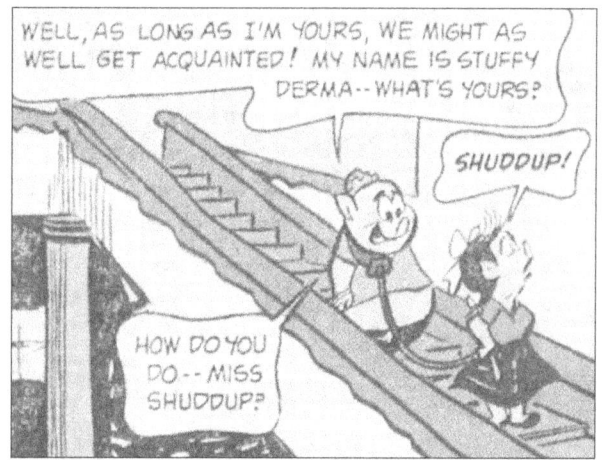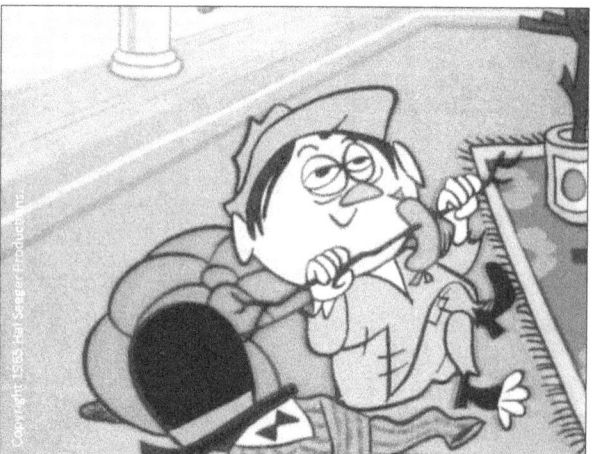

Left, Stuffy Derma, as he appeared in the form of a pig in a 1953 comic book series. Right, Stuffy Durma as he appeared in "The Milton the Monster Show." *Copyright 1965 Hal Seeger Productions.*

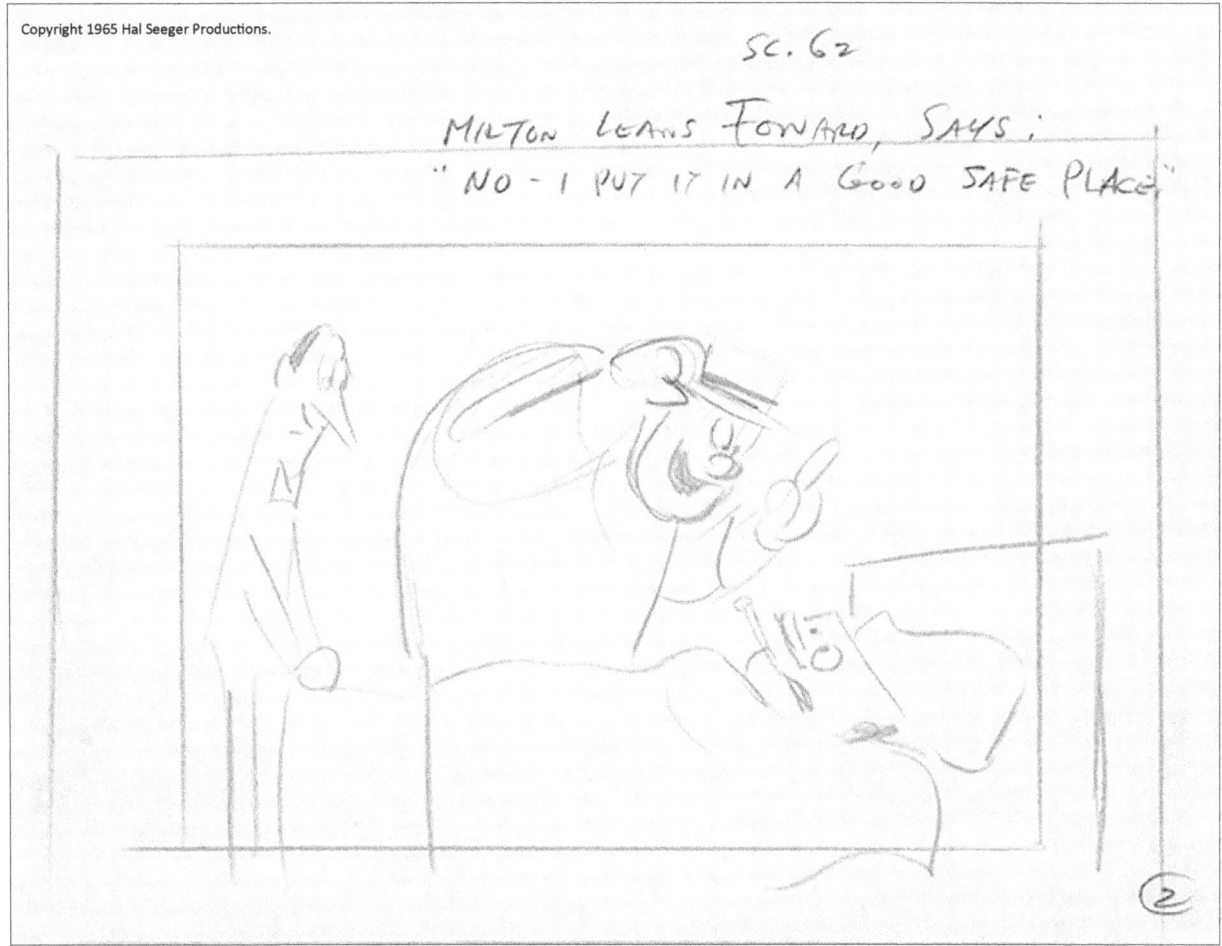

SC. 62

MILTON LEANS FOWARD, SAYS:
"NO - I PUT IT IN A GOOD SAFE PLACE"

Original sketch for the ending of the Milton the Monster episode "Who Do Voodoo?" *Copyright 1965 Hal Seeger Productions.*

Larry Best, and Beverly Arnold, Seeger's wife.

When "The Milton the Monster Show" made its debut on ABC Television October 9, 1965, it was compared to, and called, a knockoff of the popular primetime live-action shows "The Munsters" and "The Addams Family." Both programs made their debut a year before Milton, but the Hal Seeger series was in the planning stages before either was broadcast. Production delays caused "The Milton the Monster Show" to debut later making it appear to be a cheap imitation.

Only one season of "The Milton the Monster Show" was produced.

While the final episode of the season aired on April 2, 1966, the program went into re-runs and last appeared on ABC television on September 8, 1968.

Twenty-six half-hour shows were produced, each show containing three cartoons. Thirty-four adventures of Milton the Monster were created. Twenty-six adventures of Fearless Fly were created. Six Muggy-Doo adventures were created. Five Flukey Luke adventures were produced. Four Stuffy Durma adventures were created. Only 3 Penny Penguin adventures were produced.

Much of what appears in "The Milton the Monster Show" is politically incorrect in modern times. It wasn't unusual for anyone in any of the cartoons featured to pick up a firearm and start shooting.

Perhaps the most bullets fired occur in the Fluke Luke adventure, "Tired Gun," where a character named Pepe the Kid Lopez shoots up everything.

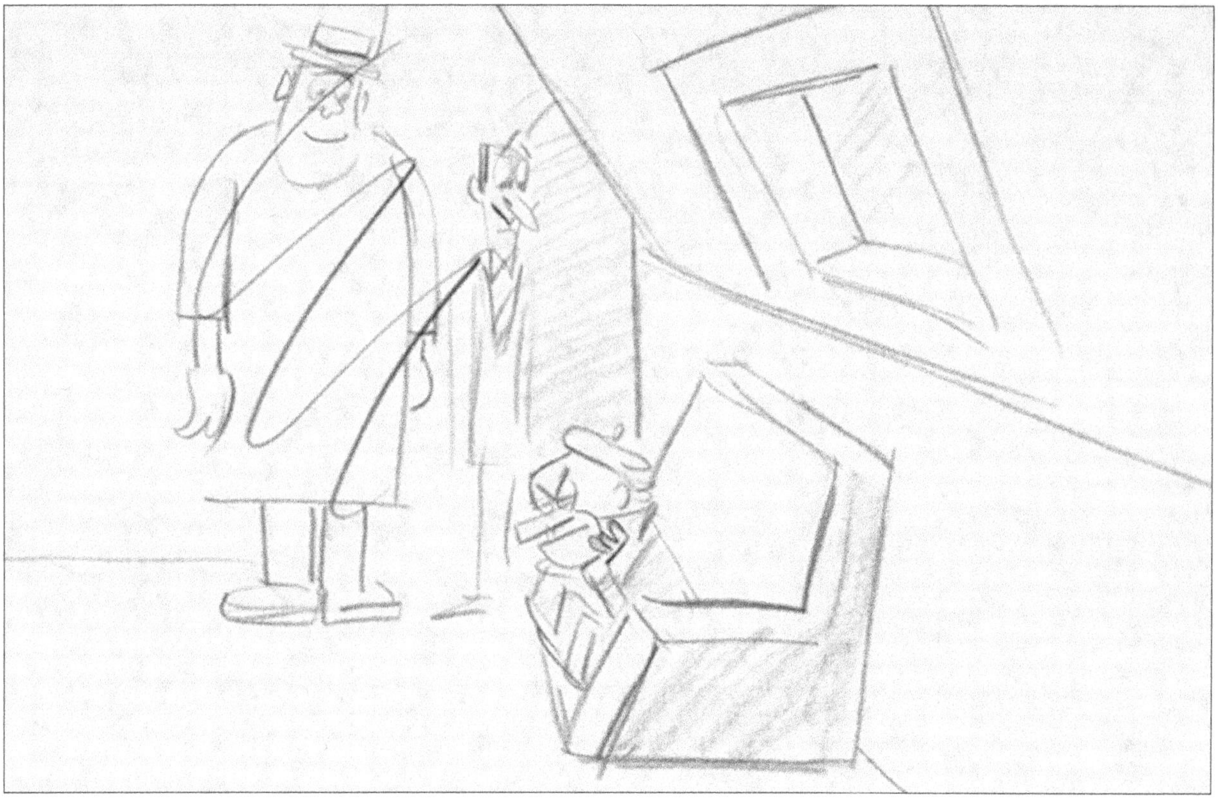

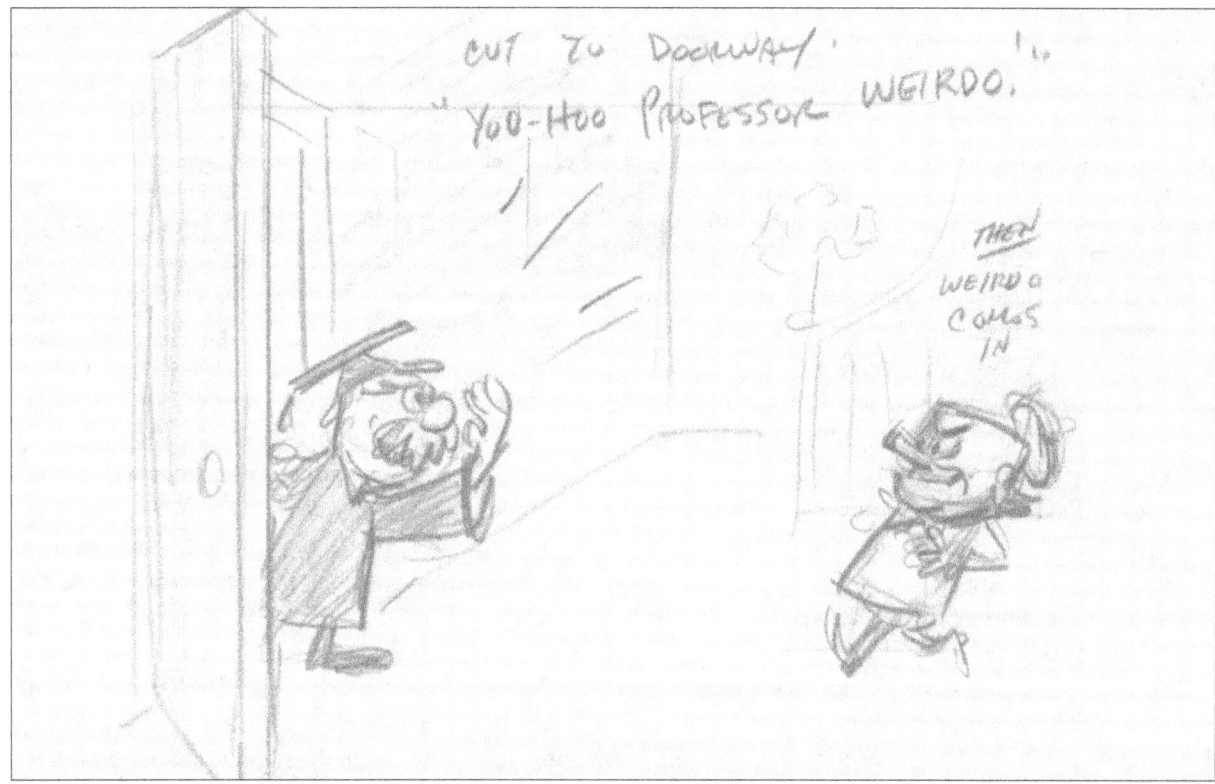

Original storyboard sketches for Milton the Monster episodes. *Copyright 1965 Hal Seeger Productions.*

Death was a common theme in Milton. Granted, it was a horror spoof. However, it wasn't unusual to hear characters plotting to take their own lives. Suicide was an occasional topic.

The supernatural was addressed as recreational at times. Séances, or speaking to the dead, was okay.

Horsey and Hiram Fly casually play with a Ouija board, with Flory in attendance, in Fearless Fly's "The Bomb's Rush" adventure.

Dr. Goo Fee and Gung Ho were stereotypical Oriental types. In fact, anyone of non-white ethnicity was often the subject of jokes or stereotypically portrayed.

Flukey Luke's Indian companion, Two Feath-ers, calls himself a "Red-skin" in their series, as Native-American jokes, were fair game.

But some critics have claimed the series pointed out such things as to present satire, or draw attention to the ridiculous nature of such comments.

In one Fearless Fly adventure, Dr. Goo Fee says to hero, "If you'll pardon my saying so, all you flies look alike."

Currently, the only DVD set available featuring the complete "The Milton the Monster Show" series was released by Shout in 2007, however, the collection has since gone out of production.

Hopefully, the Hal Seeger series will be exhumed and brought back to life sometime soon.

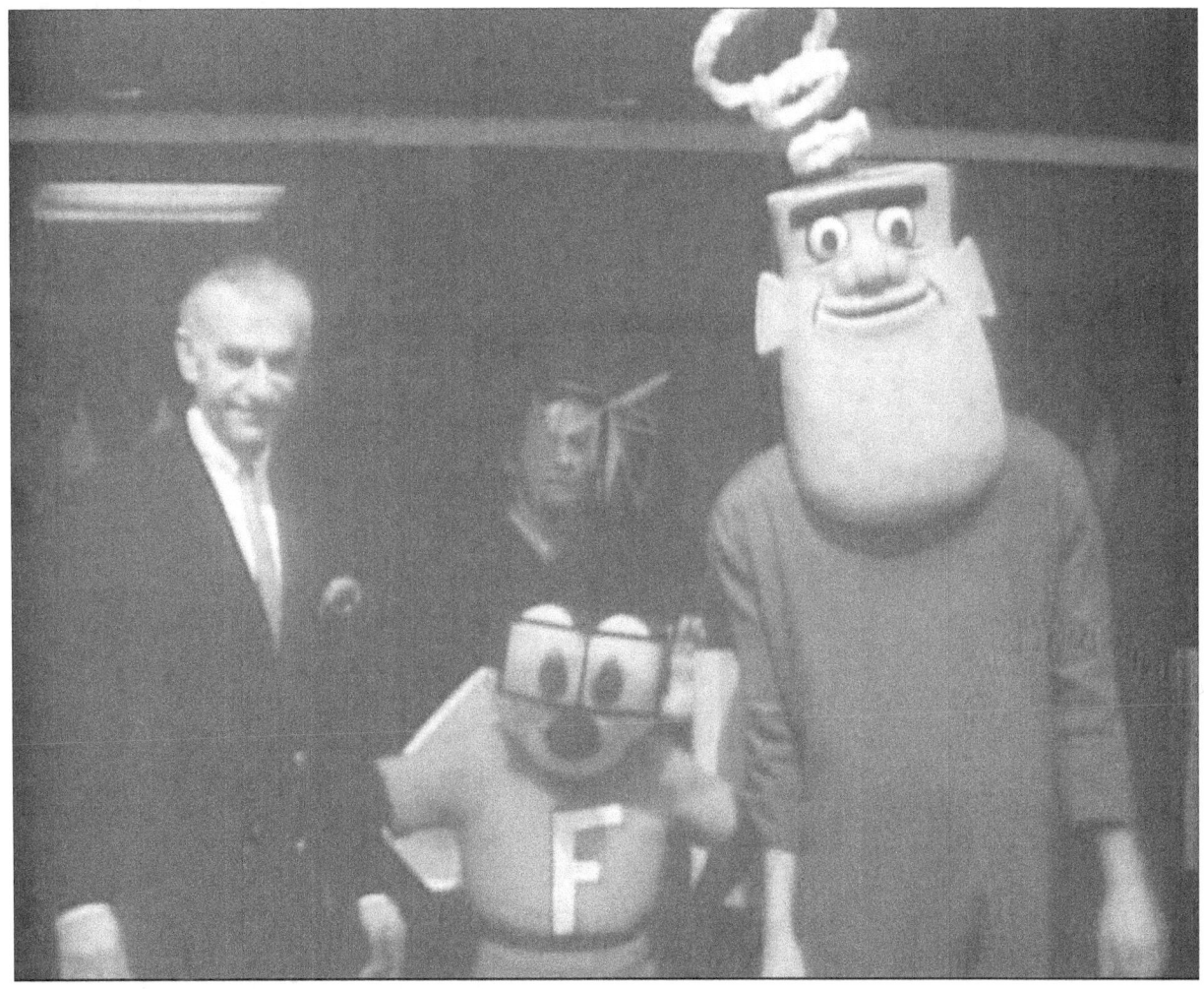

Hal Seeger, with Fearless Fly, and Milton the Monster (men is costume), on a promotional tour at the New York City Toy Fair. *Copyright 1965 Hal Seeger Productions.*

Milton the Monster in "Zelda the Zombie"

Professor Weirdo goes to war with Professor Fruitcake. Losing the conflict, Weirdo calls for a ceasefire. To ensure a treaty, Count Kook suggests a marriage between the two families will keep the peace. Thus, Milton, Heebie and Jeebie court Fruitcake's female creation, Zelda the Zombie, vying for her affection. A song, "Three Ghastly Monsters" sung by the trio fails to do the trick. Zelda wants to marry Count Kook. When Kook refuses to wed the creature, the battle resumes with him in the middle as a target of both. The bombing ceases when he promises to "go steady" with Zelda.

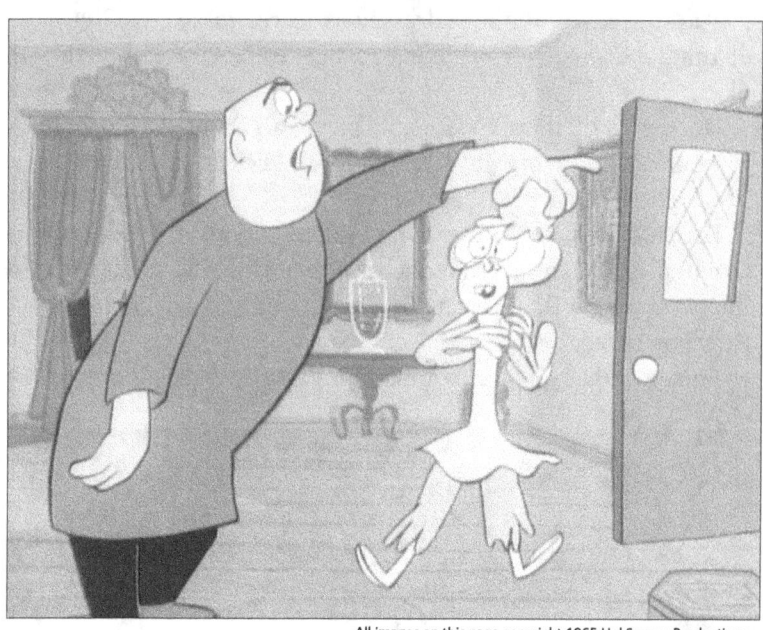

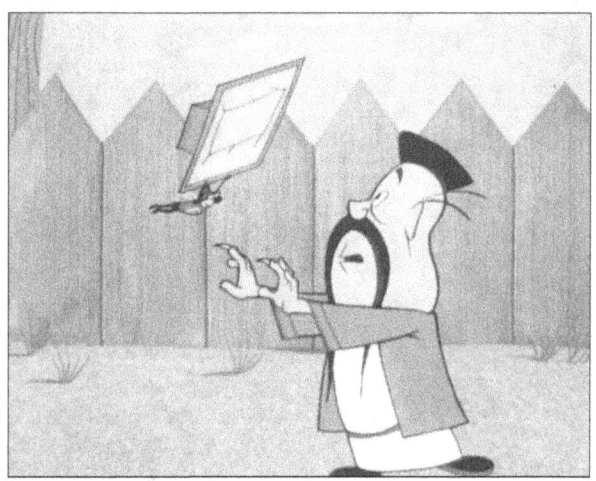

Fearless Fly in "Trick or Treatment"

Hiram Fly loses a soda drinking contest with Horsey but gains a tummy ache. Dr. Goo Fee arrives offering his services as a medical doctor. His assistant Gung Ho take Hiram to his Arizona retreat to recuperate with plans to lure Fearless Fly to the scene and capture him in a super-strong flypaper of his invention. Goo Fee momentarily succeeds in his sticky plan, but the winged hero breaks free and chases the villains away.

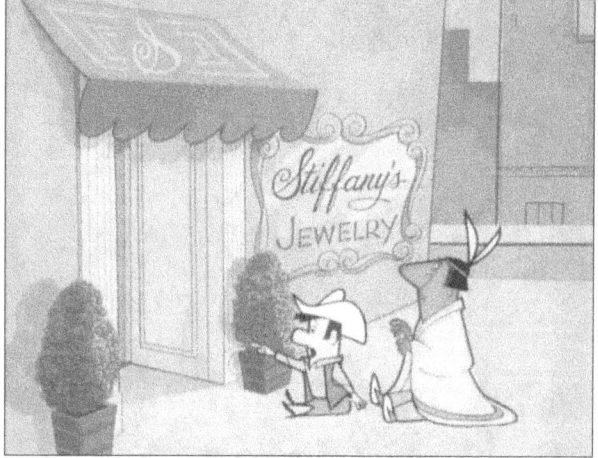

Flukey Luke in "Loot Pursuit"

Mob boss Spider Web hatches a twofold plan with his gang, to take out Flukey Luke while stealing The Hopeless Diamond. Luke renders the attackers unconscious. Luke, Two Feathers, and Pronto head out to stop the boss-man. Arriving at the Stiffany's Jewelry store hold-up, the heroes give chase, taking a shortcut through the subway. Luke causes Spider Web to crash his getaway car. The diamond is recovered and returned.

Milton the Monster in "Boy Meets Ghoul"

Professor Weirdo wants to rid himself of Milton, who has failed to do anything destructive. Weirdo devises a plan to award Heebie and Jeebie with good conduct awards, leaving Milton out, believing the disappointed monster will leave home. It fails. Weirdo tries to marry Milton off, arranging a date through newspaper classifieds. But his new gal pal, Miss Peaches, calls the wedding off after a misunderstanding. In the end, the Professor doesn't drive Milton away, and bridal plans go forward at the castle, with Weirdo mixing up a new recipe to create a bride for the groom.

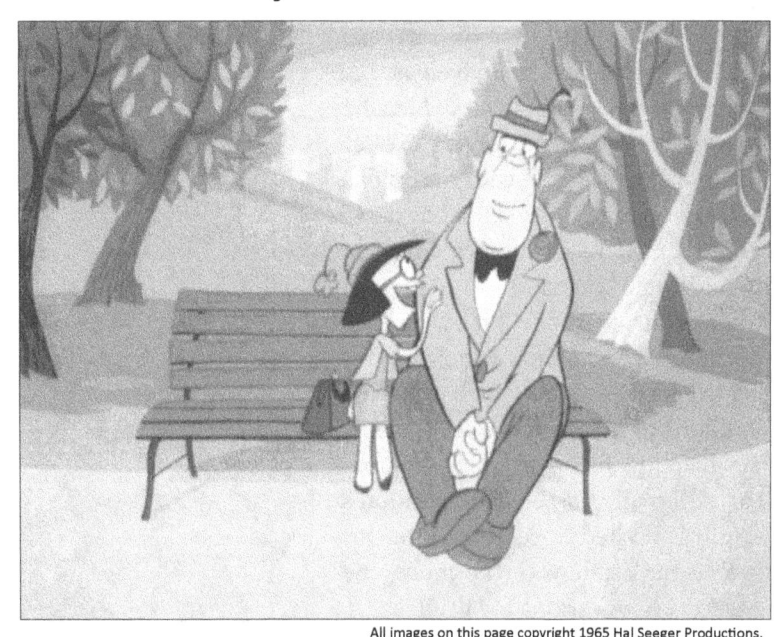

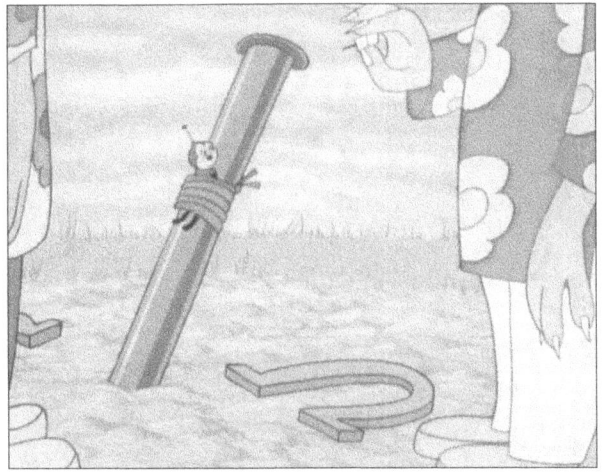

Fearless Fly in "Horse Shoo Fly"

Fearless Fly's girlfriend is excited the hero has accepted an invitation to go to the dance, but Dr. Goo Fee has different plans. He kidnaps Flory to use as bait to lure the hero to his Florida oceanside retreat. Fearless Fly arrives at the location, but surrenders upon seeing Flory's life placed in peril. Goo Fee ties Fearless Fly to a horseshoe stake and engages in a match with Gung Ho. The hero escapes the trap and defeats the terrible two.

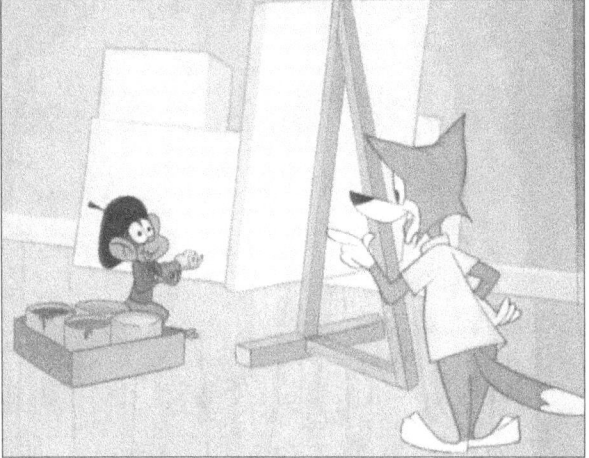

Muggy-Doo in "Gogh Van Gogh"

The Van Schmeer Gallery of Modern Art is hosting a public exhibition of the artist Simeon. Muggy-Doo thinks the paintings are junk. The artist arrives and is revealed to all to be a chimp who paints with his feet. But, the guests still rave over the abstract art, bidding a fortune for the monkey-business. Muggy-Doo wants a piece of the action and steals an organ grinder monkey. He teaches him paint, with disastrous results.

21

Milton the Monster in "Monster for Hire"

Professor Weirdo is in a financial fix. His landlord has arrived at the castle to collect the rent, which he doesn't have. Weirdo decides to offer his monsters for hire with intentions of raising much-needed money. He and Count Kook go to town advertising his new business. The promotional tour gets one hit. Milton is hired out, but in short order it is revealed he has taken a job with the landlord to help evict Weirdo, Kook, Heebie, and Jeebie from the premises. Although tossed out, Milton's family is invited back, as the monster rented the castle with the money he earned when working for Fruitcake.

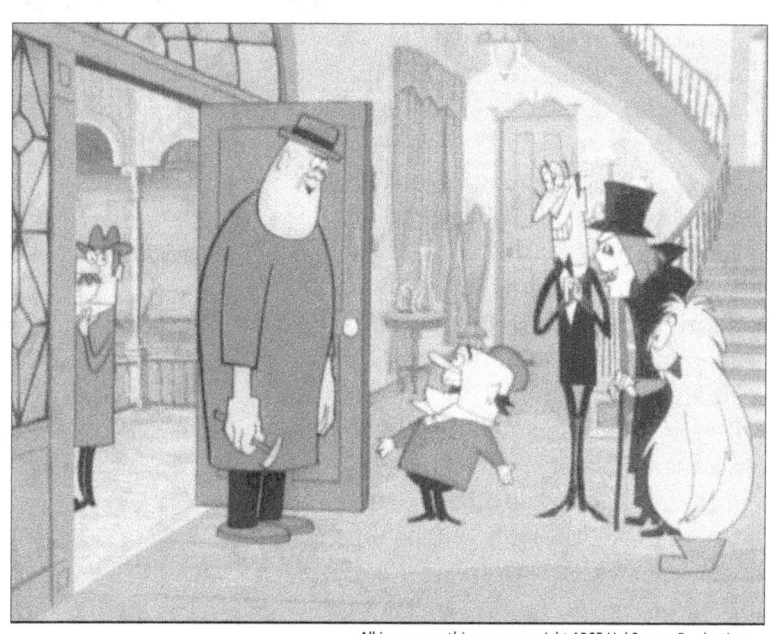

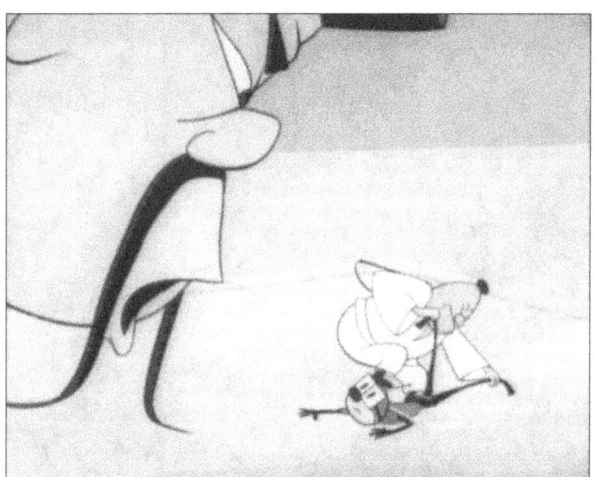

Fearless Fly in "Fatty Karate"

Dr. Goo Fee plans to use the flyweight division Judo Champion of the world, Fatty Karate, to take out Fearless Fly. Goo Fee and Gung Ho deposit Fatty Karate at the Sugar Bowl, hangout of Hiram Fly and his pals. Hiram transforms to Fearless Fly and accepts a challenge to face Karate in a match at Goo Fee's castle in Tibet. Coached on by Flory and Horsey, Fearless escapes defeat after recovering his glasses, with Karate down for the count.

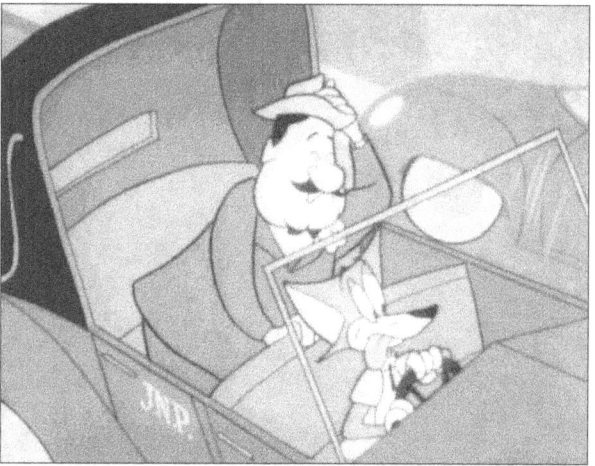

Muggy-Doo in "You Auto Be in Pictures"

Repo men arrive at Muggy Doo's Hollywood publicity office, taking his office furniture for non-payment. Left without a business, Muggy takes a job as a chauffeur for Paranoid Pictures' president. He ends up at the studio racing through the sets of several motion pictures during filming, producing excellent action scenes. Muggy is offered a job as the chief publicity man. He is jailed instead for lingering, outstanding bills.

Milton the Monster in "Who Do Voodoo?"

Professor Fruitcake stirs things up when he creates a voodoo doll of Professor Weirdo. Fruitcake shows up at the castle and makes clear his intentions of killing Weirdo, using the doll, if he fails to pay a ransom. Weirdo refuses, and Count Kook helps him prepare for his demise. The task includes placing the still-kicking Weirdo in a coffin and carrying it to the cemetery for a funeral and burial. Fruitcake shows up during the ceremony and offers to sell the voodoo doll to Weirdo at a discount. Fruitcake settles for $5 and hands the doll to Milton the Monster, which proves to be reckless.

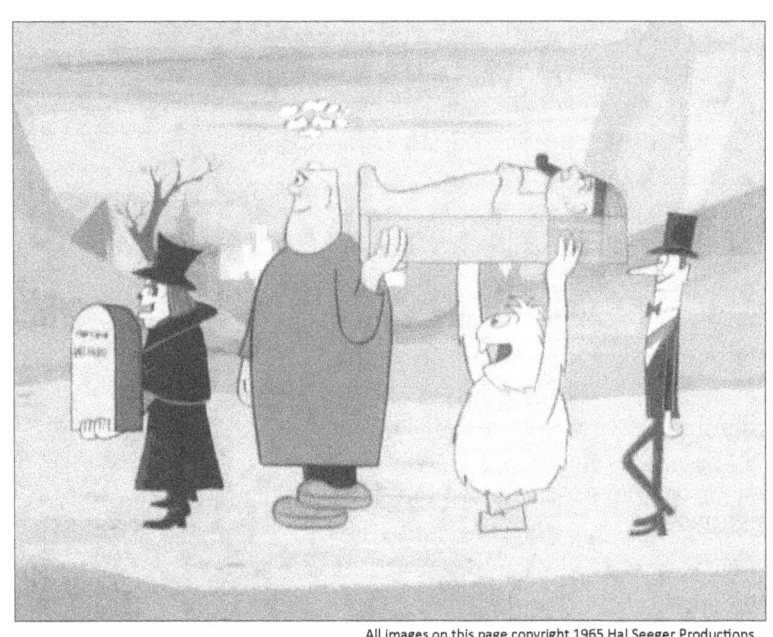

All images on this page copyright 1965 Hal Seeger Productions.

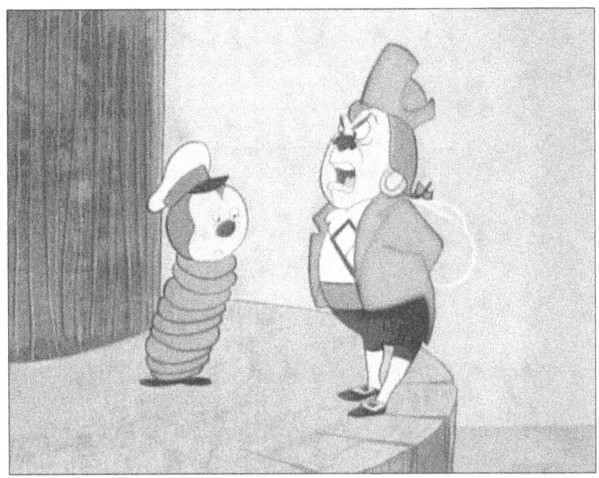

Fearless Fly in "Captain Fligh"

Dr. Goo Fee and Gung Ho sail to America in the Imperial Yacht to invite Fearless Fly on a cruise. Thinking his enemies want to make amends, the hero agrees. Goo Fee picks up a passenger along the way, Captain Fligh, a pint-sized version of Captain Bligh. Fearless is helpless against Bligh, upon losing his glasses, and forced to walk the plank. Recovering his spectacles, Fearless conducts a daring mutiny, defeating the nasty bunch.

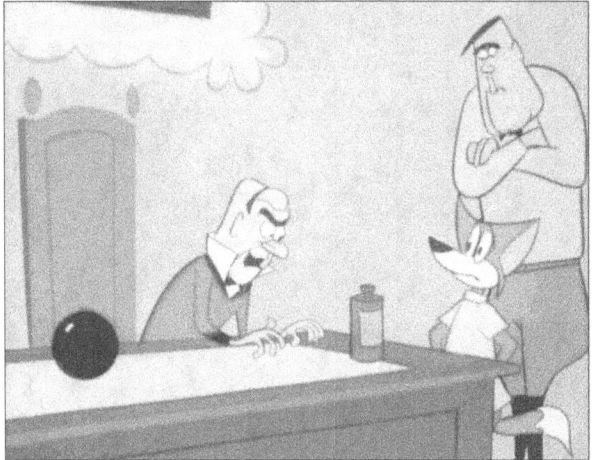

Muggy-Doo in "Muggy Doo or Die"

Working as a door-to-door vacuum cleaner salesman, Muggy arrives at the residence of monster mobsters, who hire him to make a special delivery. Conducting the drop, Muggy gets caught in a Federal Espionage Agency sting operation. The Feds make him a counterspy. Muggy returns to the criminal lair, but is exposed and locked up. He uses a transmitter, pinpointing his location for the Feds, bringing an end to the sordid operation.

Milton the Monster in "The Pot Thickens"

Professor Weirdo gets a letter from his Aunt Hagatha, a witch, announcing her plans to pay a visit to his castle on Horror Hill. Hagatha wants to meet the monsters, but Weirdo isn't too sure about exposing her to his flawed creation, Milton. If Auntie sees him, she may not divulge her secret monster-making recipes. Seeking to remove Milton from the scenario, Weirdo and Count Kook dump him off at the North Pole. Hagatha arrives and meets Heebie and Jeebie without issue. When Milton shows up, Hagatha likes him. Her recipe, however, is for spaghetti and meatballs.

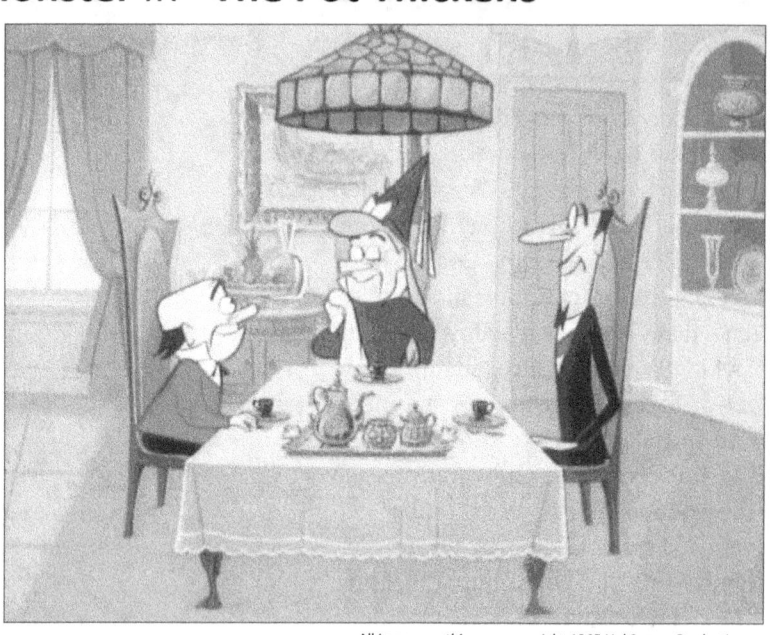

All images on this page copyright 1965 Hal Seeger Productions.

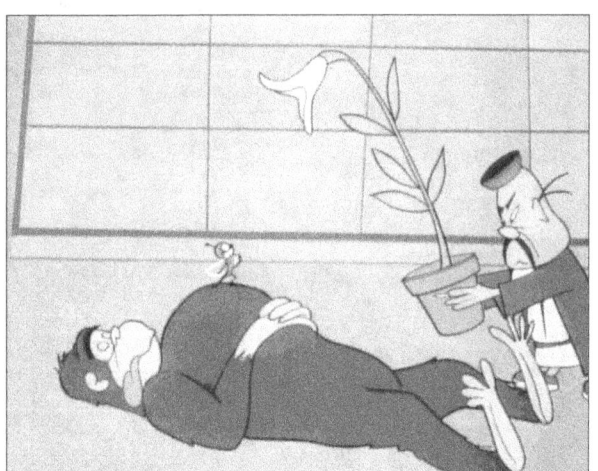

Fearless Fly in "The Goofy Doctor Goo Fee"

Dr. Goo Fee wants to add Fearless Fly to his unique collection of caged creatures. He dispatches Gung Ho to capture the hero and bring him back to his castle. Gung Ho returns with the target, but it turns out to be Horsey the Fly, dressed in a Fearless Fly outfit for a costume party. The real Fearless Fly comes to the rescue and battles the Abominable Snowman, a killer gorilla, and a man-eating plant before freeing his friend.

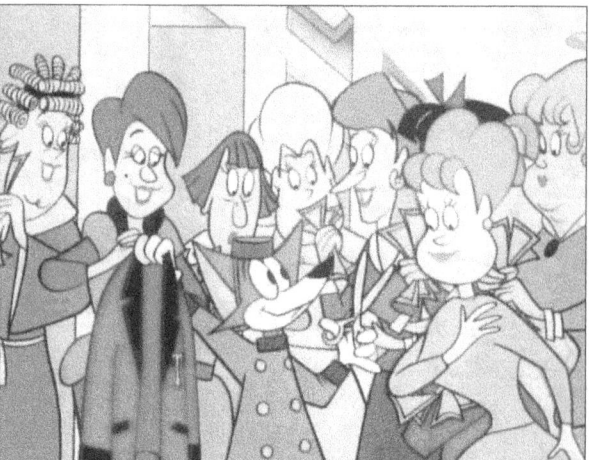

Muggy-Doo in "Rags to Riches"

Muggy-Doo takes a job as a hotel bellhop and witnesses ladies ripping the clothing off Hollywood star, Tag Ending, in the lobby. Muggy concludes that he can make more money selling souvenirs taken from celebrity guests. Muggy befriends Tag and engages in stealing his personal belongings and items from his room. Muggy even assumes the celebrity's identity and gets mobbed himself. A policeman puts an end to the scam.

Milton the Monster in "Medium Undone"

Professor Weirdo fears a ghost has taken up residence in his castle and calls everyone together to conduct a séance. Using a crystal ball, Weirdo attempts to summon the spirit. A ghost arrives at the door and is allowed in. The spirit announces it is the ghost of Professor Fruitcake. However, it is a ruse. Fruitcake is simply donning a sheet and wants a payoff to make the ghost vanish. Professor Weirdo, Count Kook, Milton, Heebie and Jeebie go to the cemetery to see if Fruitcake is truly dead, and engage in digging up his grave, where they find him very much alive in his coffin.

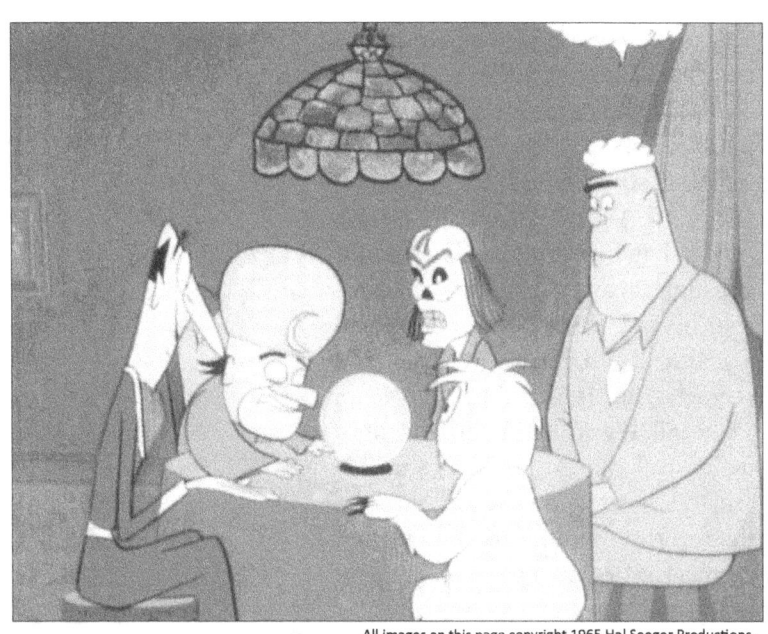

All images on this page copyright 1965 Hal Seeger Productions.

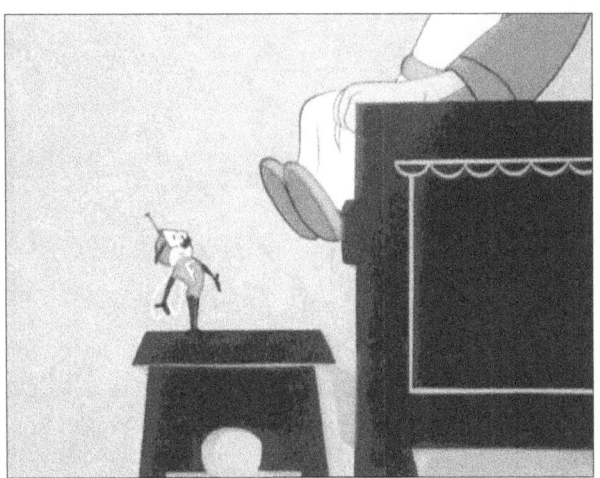

Fearless Fly in "Sly Fly"

Dr. Goo Fee is about to sacrifice himself in his mountaintop castle, but changes his mind and recruits Gung Ho to fly a kamikaze mission to Hiram Fly's matchbox, diving his plane into the residence. Failing in his mission, Fearless Fly flies Gung Ho back to Tibet to face Goo Fee. The Dr. spares Ho's life and invites Fearless Fly to stay as an overnight guest. An attempt to bomb Fearless fails and Goo Fee and Gung Ho suffer dishonor.

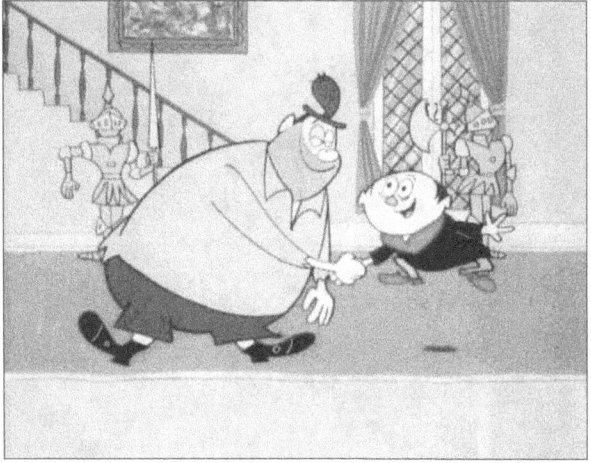

Stuffy Durma in "From Wrecks to Riches"

The millionaire Hobo makes his debut with old hobo pal, Stu Mulligan, showing up at his residence. Durma's assistant and dedicated guide, Bradley Brinkley, disapproves of the guest. He helps Stuffy get ready for a business meeting with Mr. Beeswax. But Durma returns to his hobo persona, causing alarm. The situation changes when Beeswax recognizes Mulligan, his old hobo pal, and gives up his job to rejoin Stu on the road.

Milton the Monster in "Monster Mutiny"

Professor Weirdo believes he has concocted an antidote to eliminate Milton's kind demeanor. He tries the potion on himself. The result is mean, nasty behavior, but the serum wears off. Weirdo mixes up a more potent batch. Afraid his boss might consume it again and become a tyrant, Count Kook devises a plan to overthrow Professor Weirdo and recruits Heebie and Jeebie to help. They jail Weirdo and throw Milton in his cell due to his loyalty to his creator. The two escape and turn the tables on the mutineers, but all find themselves locked up in the dungeon in the end.

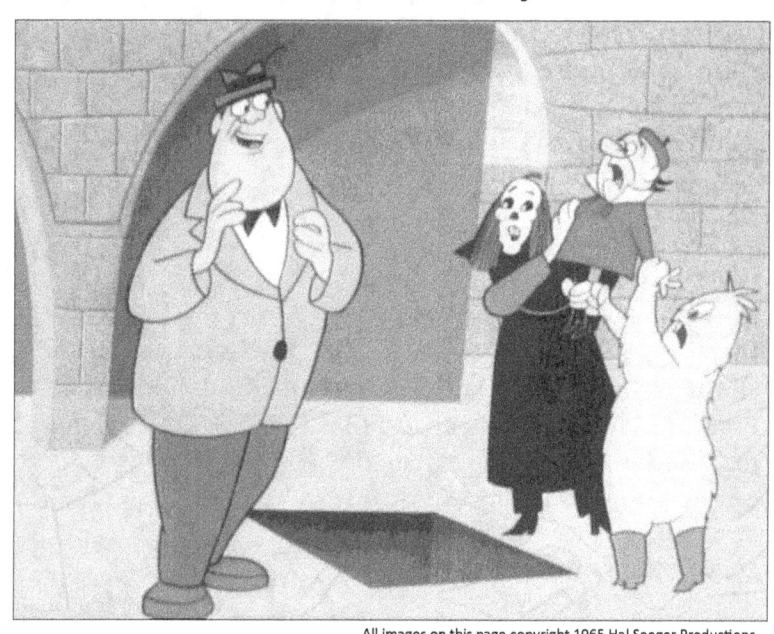

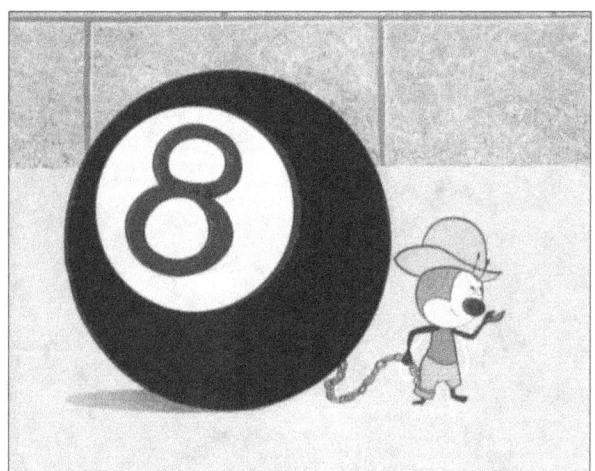

Fearless Fly in "Throne for a Loss"

Dr. Goo Fee hatches a plan to bribe Hiram the Fly to destroy Fearless Fly and show evidence of his demise for a reward. Goo Fee dispatches Gung Ho to the Sugar Bowl, where he pitches the offer. Hiram plays along as if he is onboard, and tricks Ho into thinking he has accomplished the task by showing him a bag containing the hero's costume and glasses. Gung Ho overthrows Goo Fee, and Hiram becomes Fearless Fly, ending the fiasco.

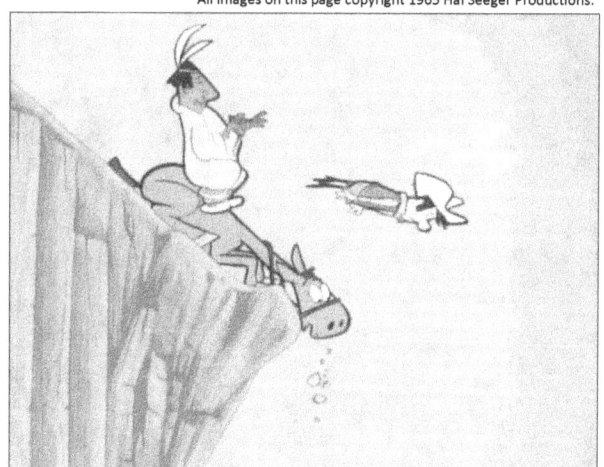

Flukey Luke in "Missing Masters"

Mob boss Spider Web hatches a plan to knock off five museums, stealing valuable works of art worth millions. His henchmen conduct the nighttime thefts without resistance. Flukey Luke, Two Feathers, and Pronto track the criminals back to Spider Web's lair. Web attempts a getaway, with Luke and company in pursuit. Luke single-handedly takes down the boss, whose truckload of art careens off a bridge into a river below.

Milton the Monster in "Ghoul School"

The secret brotherhood of monsters, comprised of Heebie and Jeebie, conducts a meeting in their clubhouse. Milton begs to join. Professor Weirdo expresses concern his monsters are becoming unmotivated slobs, so invites Aunt Hagatha to the castle to teach the trio etiquette and manners. Heebie and Jeebie can't stand the arrangement, and tell Milton if he gets Hagatha to move out of the castle he will be welcomed into their secret organization. Milton succeeds, but the plan backfires. Aunt Hagatha has moved from the main residence into the monster's clubhouse, imposing her authority there.

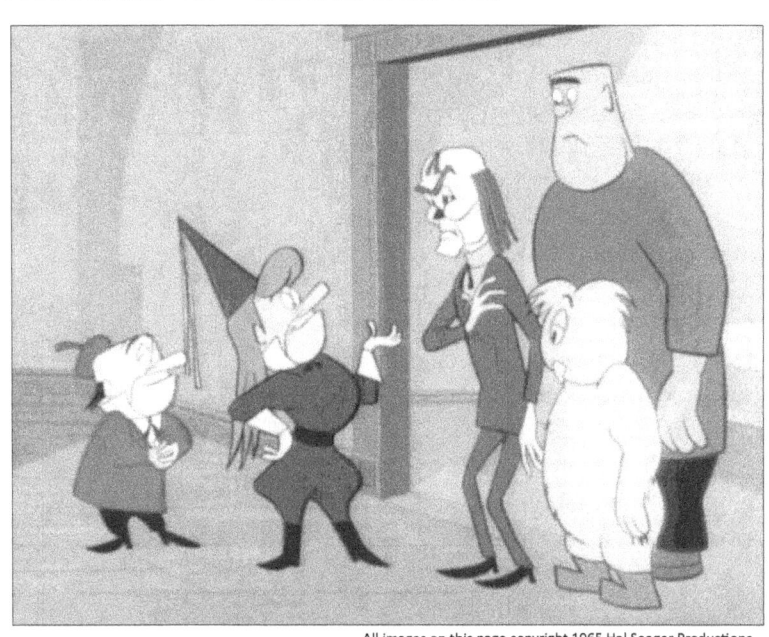

All images on this page copyright 1965 Hal Seeger Productions.

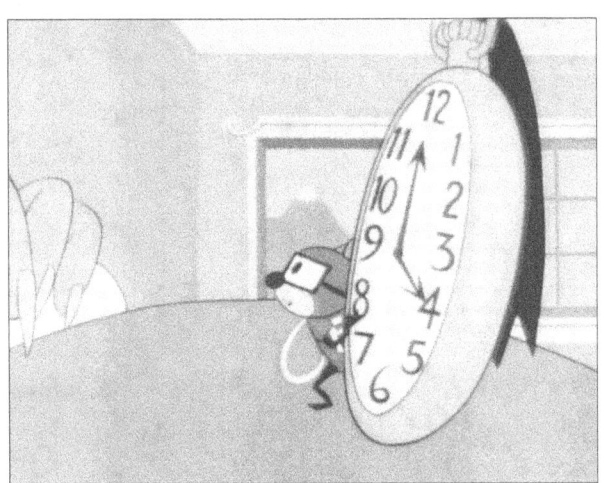

Fearless Fly in "The Bomb's Rush"

Hiram Fly is surprised when Gung Ho arrives at the Sugar Bowl to announce Dr. Goo Fee is on his deathbed and wants to make amends with Fearless Fly. The hero flies to Goo Fee's castle in Tibet to be at the wizard's side. It is a ruse to lure Fearless to his death. Goo Fee gives Fearless a gold watch that is a time bomb, but the plan backfires on the master and his assistant. The clock explodes, ending the fiasco.

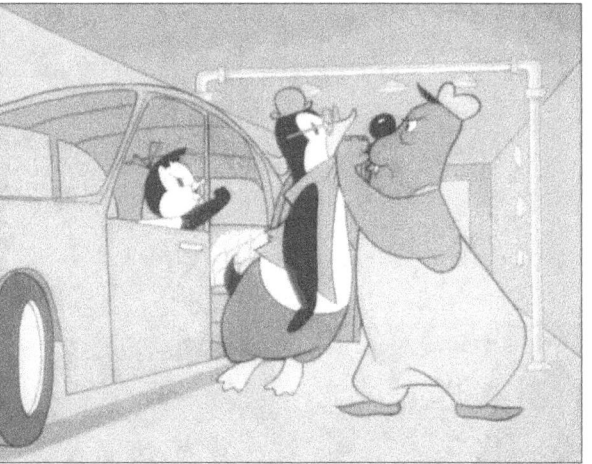

Penny Penguin in "There Auto Be a Law"

In Penny Penguin's debut, she puts her daddy, who wants to wash his car, through a series wet predicaments. She hooks the water hose up to a washing machine, with disastrous results. Penny accompanies her daddy to the car wash next, and rolls down the vehicle's windows, flooding the interior. Placing the car on a hydraulic lift for servicing leads to the attendant being clobbered, and he awarding daddy two black eyes.

Milton the Monster in "Hector the Protector"

Professor Weirdo is disappointed Milton has failed to do anything rotten, so devises plans to get rid of him. Weirdo holds a public raffle, the door prize being Milton. However, Milton has the winning number and returns home. Weirdo advertises Milton for sale in the newspaper and criminal extortionist Hector the Protector purchases the monster. Hector sends Milton out to collect protection money from unwilling clients. Milton collects from one individual then gives it away to another, who is down on his luck. Furious, Hector charges the castle, shoots up the place and drops Milton off.

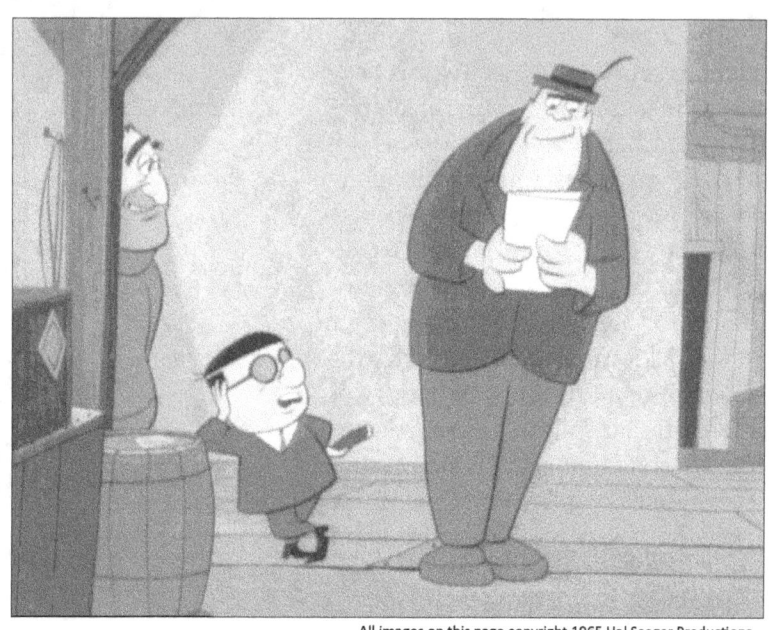

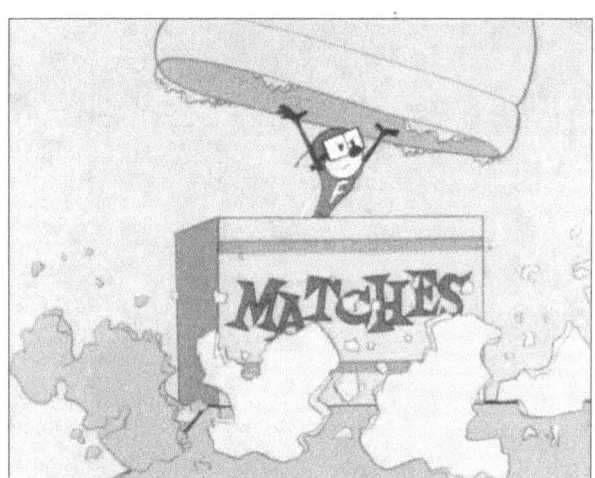

Fearless Fly in "Fly Hijack"

Dr. Goo Fee and Gung Ho travel to America and pitch a tent outside Hiram Fly's matchbox residence, in order to catch Fearless Fly. Hiram dons his Fearless Fly attire and investigates. He determines his new neighbors are harmless. But when they steal Hiram's matchbox, taking it back to Tibet, it lures the hero to Goo Fee's lair. Goo Fee's attempt to entomb Fearless, by cementing the box onto the base of a statue, fails.

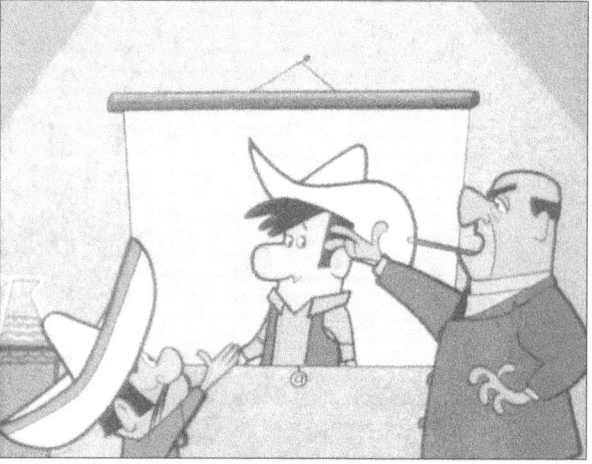

Flukey Luke in "Tired Gun"

Aware his henchmen are afraid to take on Flukey Luke, mob boss, Spider Web, recruits hired gun, Pepe the Kid Lopez. Spider explains to Pepe he must get rid of Flukey Luke so his plans to empty an armored truck of its riches will be successful. They pull off the heist, placing bags of cash into Spider's limo, but his associates flee in fear and Pepe takes the wheel. Pepe can't drive and crashes the car, ending the scenario.

Milton the Monster in "Horrorbaloo"

A meeting of the secret brotherhood of monsters commences in an underground cave. A motion is made to elect a new president, replacing Heebie. When the ballots are counted, Heebie claims he is the winner. Disapproving of the result, Milton and Abercrombie depart and start a second monster club, leaving Heebie and Jeebie behind. Both clubs compete to woo Fangenstein to join their organization. Fangenstein stops the bickering by consolidating both clubs, appointing himself president, then kicks all members out. The rejected quartet is forced to use a dilapidated shack as a clubhouse.

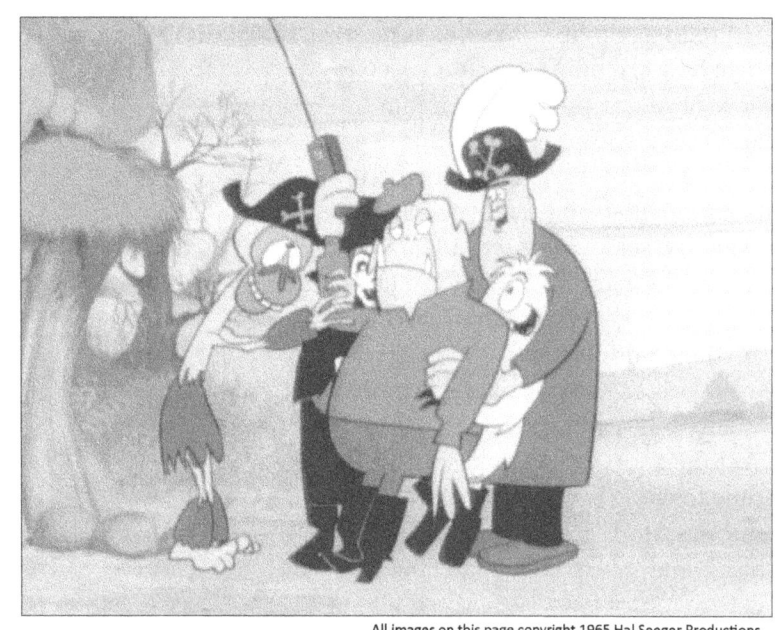

All images on this page copyright 1965 Hal Seeger Productions.

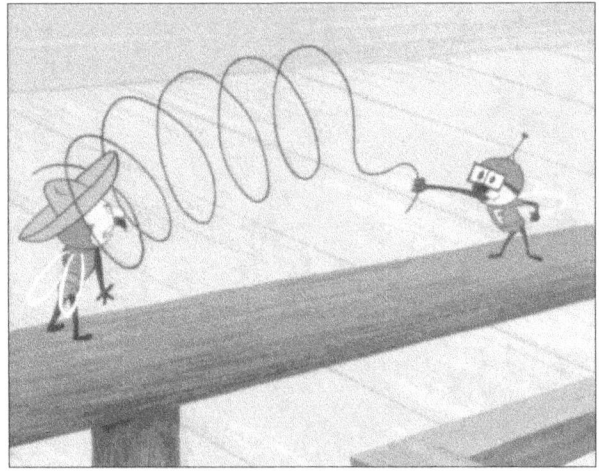

Fearless Fly in "Si Si Fly"

Dr. Goo Fee goes on vacation, taking Gung Ho with him to Mexico. But first, the two stop at Fearless Fly's residence and invite him to come along. The holiday is over when Fearless is placed in a ring and faces a bullfight. However, the bull takes off after Gung Ho. Fearless comes to the rescue and takes down the animal. Next Fearless faces Si Si Fly, a whip-wielding bad hombre. Fearless defeats Si Si and ties him up, using the whip.

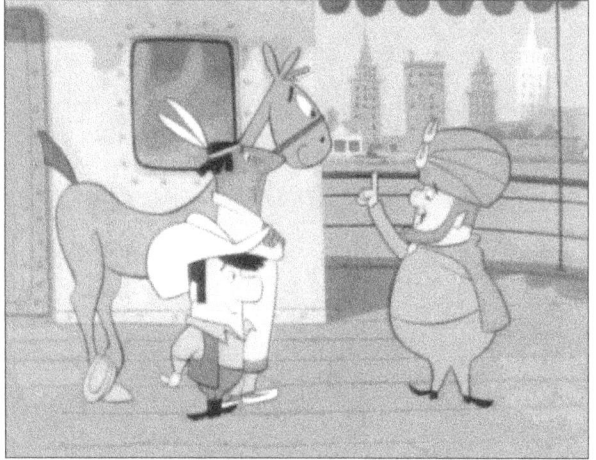

Flukey Luke in "Palace Malice"

A prince arrives at an American port and is greeted by an ambassador, who assures the man the promise of a million dollar loan for his tiny, impoverished country. But the ambassador and a general to the prince have plans to steal the money. A giant hulk named Gung Ho is dispatched to take out Luke, but the cowboy, Two Feathers and Pronto disrupt the schemers, and seize the loan money, so it can be presented to the prince.

Milton the Monster in "Goon Platoon"

Professor Weirdo receives a message that Milton, Heebie, and Jeebie have been accepted for service in the army. The trio packs up and arrives at the military base, taking up occupancy in the monster platoon division barracks. Sergeant Adam discovers the recruits present a daunting challenge. War games become anything but playtime, when the trio mistakes an army colonel for the enemy and captures him. Professor Weirdo and Count Kook have little time to enjoy being empty-nesters as the monsters are kicked out of the army and given their marching orders to return home.

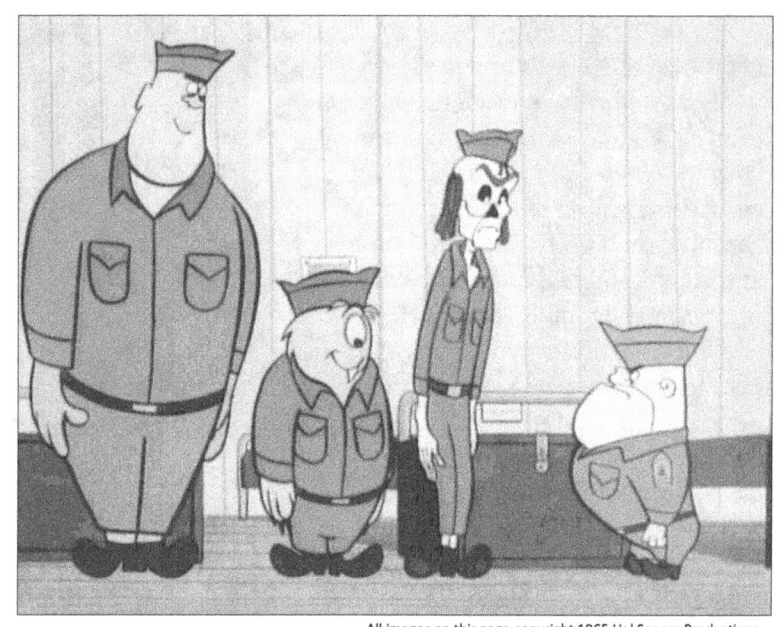

All images on this page copyright 1965 Hal Seeger Productions.

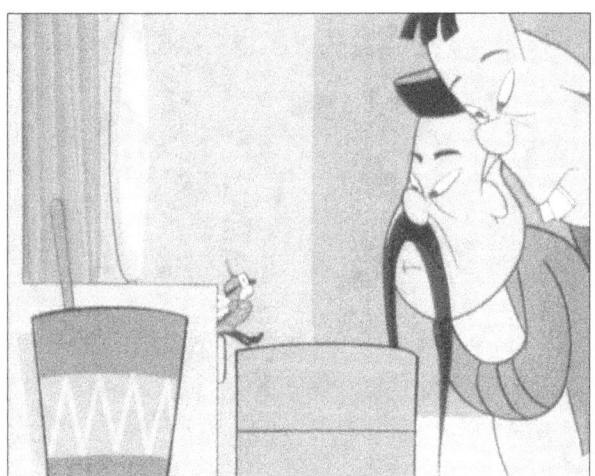

Fearless Fly in "The House-Fly Guest"

Dr. Goo Fee announces he is stepping down from the throne to retire. His assistant, Gung Ho, must prove he is worthy of assuming the throne, by capturing Fearless Fly and bringing him to the castle. Gung Ho arrives at the Sugar Bowl and asks Hiram if he can pose as Fearless Fly to show his master. Once in the castle, Fearless is invited to stay overnight. Goo Fee tries to destroy him, but in the end, Fearless assumes the throne.

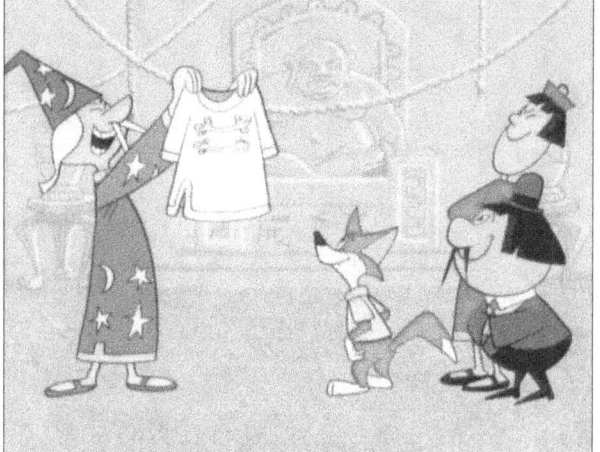

Muggy-Doo in "Fortune Kooky"

An aged Chinese wizard sees in the stars the new year shall be the year of the fox. The wizard and his assistants bump into Muggy-Doo and believe he is the chosen one. Muggy gets to don the sacred golden jacket. The assistants want the valuable coat and steal it away. Muggy gives chase in a rickshaw and recovers the jacket, but is required to give it up. The wizard has made an error. It is supposed to be the year of the chimpanzee.

30

Milton the Monster in "The Dummy Talks"

Milton surprises his family when he demonstrates his new ventriloquist, attaching a string to the mouth of a shrunken head. The tugging of the string loosens the artifact's jaw, enabling him to speak on his own. The head requests a body. Weirdo places the noggin' in the helmet of a suit of armor. The angry knight seeks revenge and targets Weirdo, whose ancestor had shrunk the head. Battle commences between the monsters and the knight. Weirdo surrenders and agrees to take a head-shrinking potion concocted by his opponent. But it is a ruse to capture the head and place it back under glass.

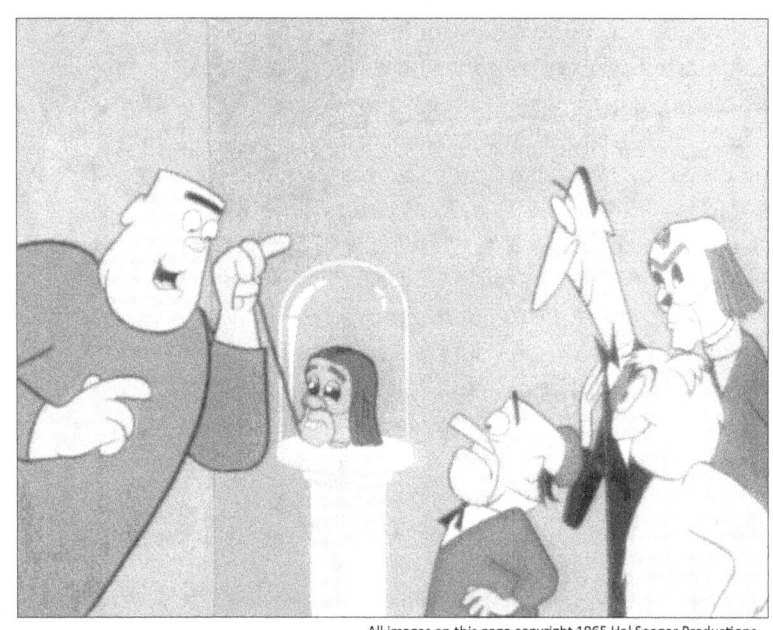

All images on this page copyright 1965 Hal Seeger Productions.

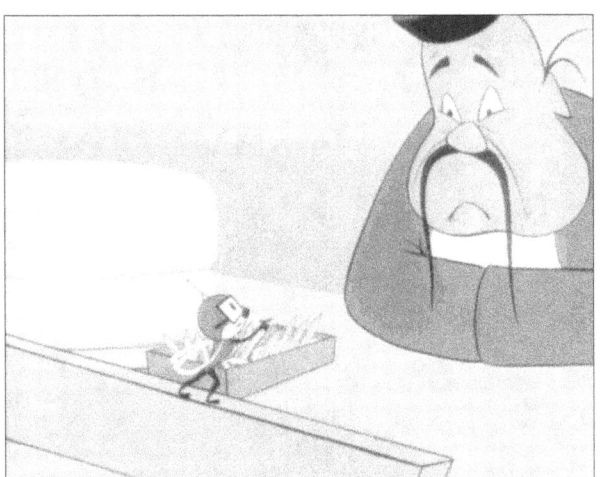

Fearless Fly in "Invincible vs. Invisible"

For his birthday, Dr. Goo Fee informs Gung Ho that he wants the rarest jewel, the greatest painting and the world's finest statue as gifts. To do this, and avoid confrontation with Fearless Fly, Gung Ho takes a potion, rendering him invisible. Gung Ho successfully steals a jeweled crown, a prized painting, and a golden flamingo statue. Fearless Fly track the items back to Goo Fee's castle, exposes Gung Ho and recovers the treasures.

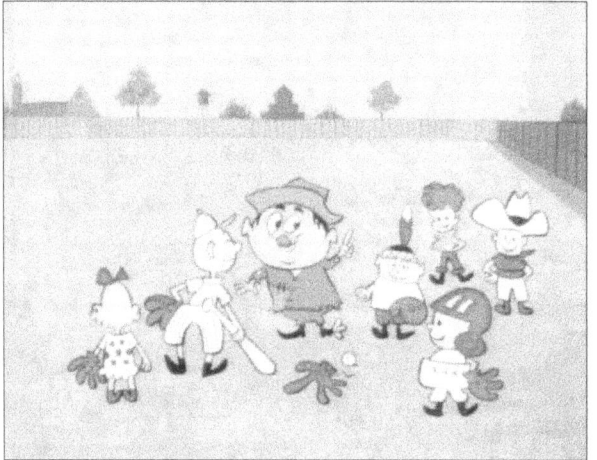

Stuffy Durma in "Suit Yourself"

Secretary Bradley Brinkley suits up Stuffy Derma for an important board meeting at Durma Incorporated. But Durma changes into his tattered attire in the limousine taking him there. He skips out of his obligation to participate in a children's softball game. Stuffy causes the destruction of the team's ball. Stuffy finds Brinkley, who suits him up again for the meeting. Afterward, Durma pawns the suit to buy a new baseball for the kids.

31

Milton the Monster in "Pie in the Sky"

Creating a new creature in his laboratory Professor Weirdo is missing a key ingredient: heavy knuckle powder. He sends Milton to borrow some from Professor Fruitcake, but returns with a black eye. Weirdo bakes an explosive pie for Fruitcake, seeking revenge, but Fruitcake dresses it up as a cake, and sends it to Weirdo, with big-bang results. Weirdo, with Heebie and Jeebie, trick Abercrombie the Zombie and hold him captive at the bottom of a well. Fruitcake captures Heebie and Jeebie, leaving Milton the last monster standing. In the end, Weirdo gets the powder and a black eye, too.

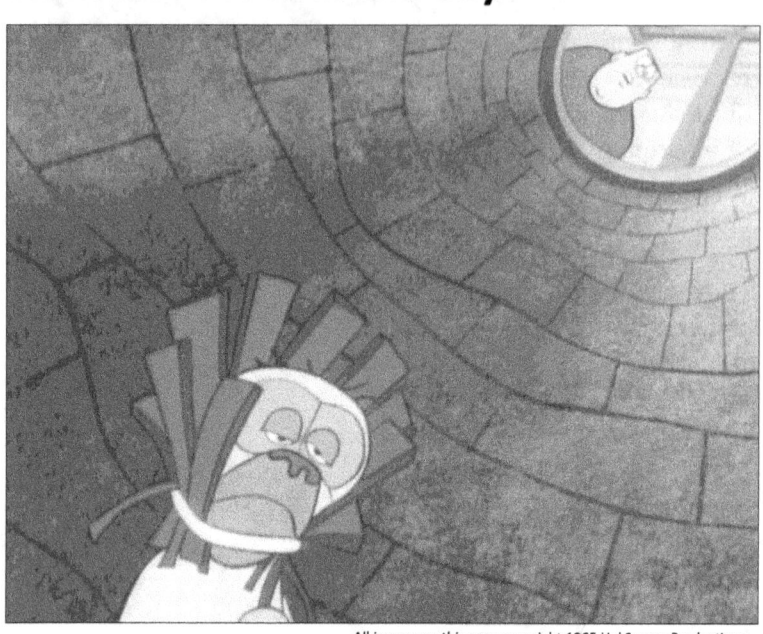

All images on this page copyright 1965 Hal Seeger Productions.

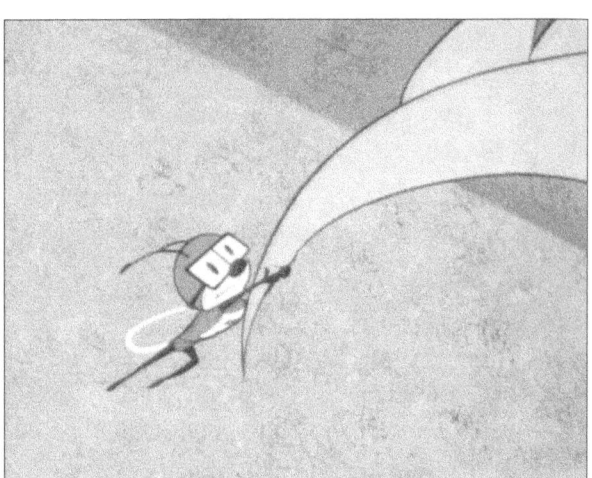

Fearless Fly in "Fly by Might"

In what is the first "Fearless Fly" adventure produced, viewers are introduced to Hiram Fly, Horsey, Flora and Professor Weirdo, who became a fixture of "Milton the Monster" tales. Weirdo uses his ray gun to transform animals into gigantic monsters to destroy the city. Fearless Fly appears on the scene to save the day. This adventure is one of three pre-"Milton the Monster" productions intended for "The Fearless Fly Show."

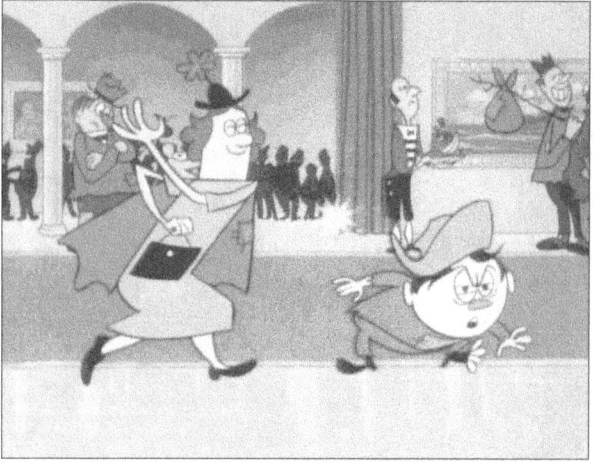

Stuffy Durma in "Hobo Hootenanny"

Stuffy Durma's assistant, Bradley Brinkley, arranges a large reception party for Maharaja Ringading and dignitaries. For amusement, he makes it a hobo costume party. It presents the perfect opportunity for Stuffy to sneak his friends, Stu Mulligan and Ashcan Annie, into his mansion and go unnoticed. Stu and Annie mingle with bigwigs, but trouble arises when Brinkley counts two more than the 100 invited to the event.

Milton the Monster in "Monstrous Escape"

Professor Weirdo is concerned Heebie and Jeebie cost him too much money residing at the castle, so he tries to sell them to Professor Fruitcake. Fruitcake inspects them, but passes on the offer. Weirdo orders Milton to lock Heebie and Jeebie in the dungeon. Subsequently, they escape and head into the city, eating at a restaurant. Having no money, the two skip out on the bill, prompting authorities to issue a bulletin to capture the thieves. Weirdo and Fruitcake hear about the fugitives, and seek to apprehend them for a reward. In conclusion, Weirdo gets stuck with the pair, again.

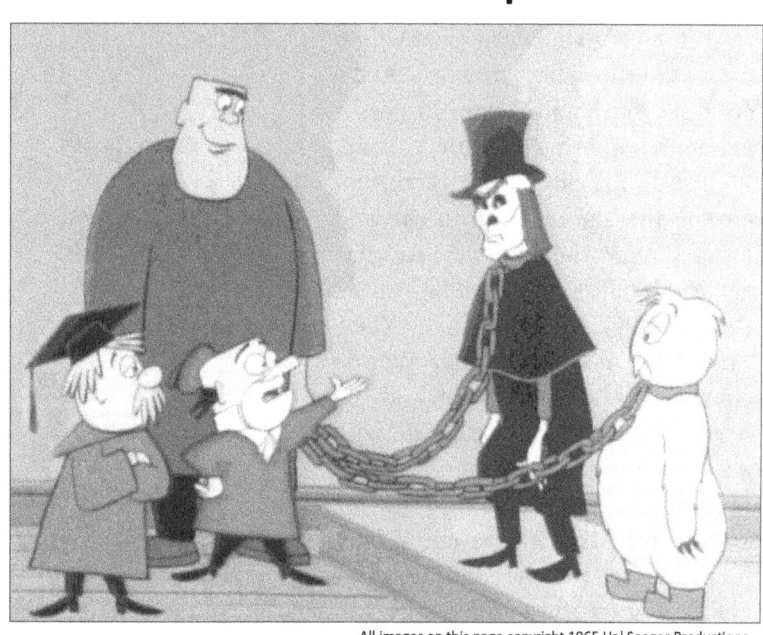

All images on this page copyright 1965 Hal Seeger Productions.

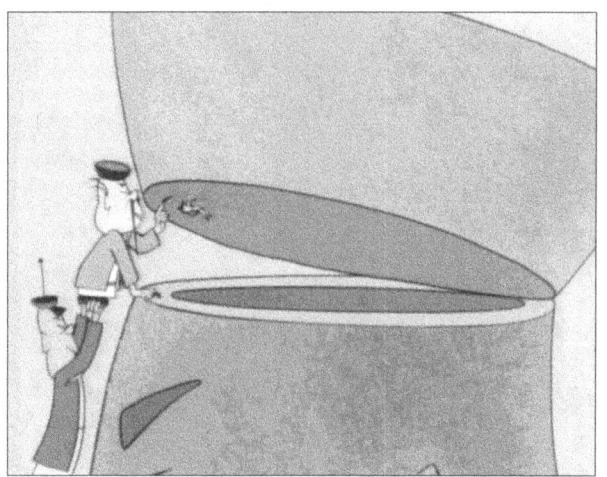

Fearless Fly in "The Sphinx Jinx"

Dr. Goo Fee believes the gods want Fearless Fly to erect a Sphinx honoring him atop Goo Fee Mountain. He and Gung Ho journey to America, where they trick Fearless into accepting it is his duty to fulfill the promise made by one of Fearless' distant ancestors. The hero builds the "Goo Fee sphinx," but it becomes his tomb. Goo Fee and Gung Ho move the sphinx head, to fix its hat, and Fearless escapes, teaching the two a lesson.

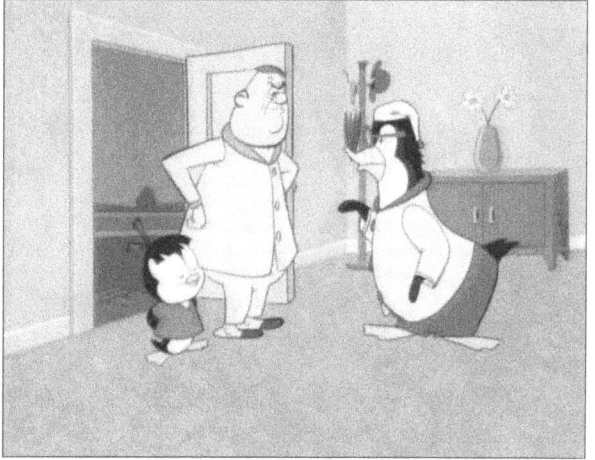

Penny Penguin in "Penny Ante"

Penny Penguin's mother allows her to ride in the car to pick up father from work. Penny pleads to visit daddy's office. There, Penny meets her dad's supervisor, Mr. Grumbly. Tension rises and concern regarding what offensive thing Penny will say to the boss. Subsequently, Penny wants 50 cents more in her allowance. Her father refuses. So, Penny intends to move in with Mr. Grumbly, resulting in her father getting a raise.

Milton the Monster in "Abercrombie the Zombie"

Milton is driving Professor Weirdo nuts. Weirdo plots to steal Abercrombie the Zombie from Professor Fruitcake, then sell Milton to him. Weirdo and Kook capture Abercrombie in the darkness of night and bring him to their castle. Fruitcake arrives the next day and tells Weirdo the zombie has vanished. Thus, Fruitcake buys Milton after Weirdo convinces him the monster is vicious. Fruitcake is displeased with his new addition, when he discovers Milton is too sweet and kind. Heebie and Jeebie send Abercrombie back to Fruitcake, for cheating at cards, and Milton returns to the castle.

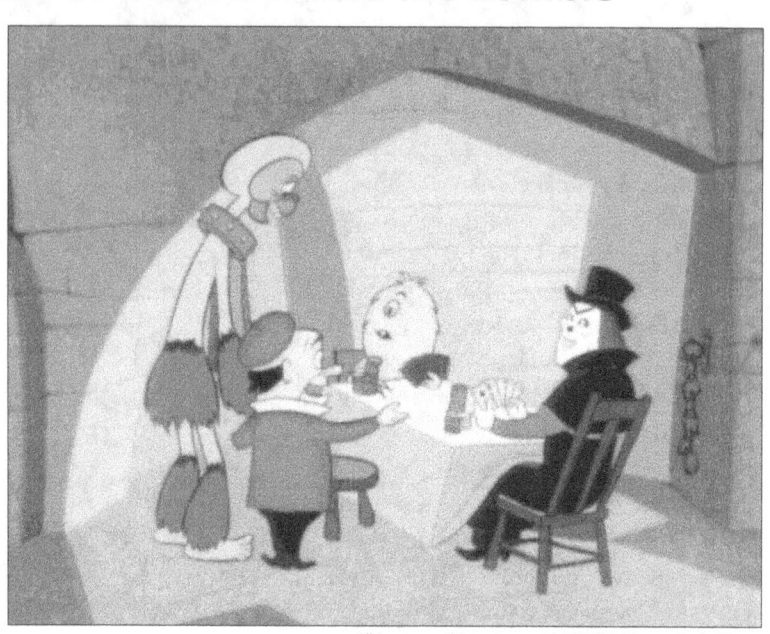

All images on this page copyright 1965 Hal Seeger Productions.

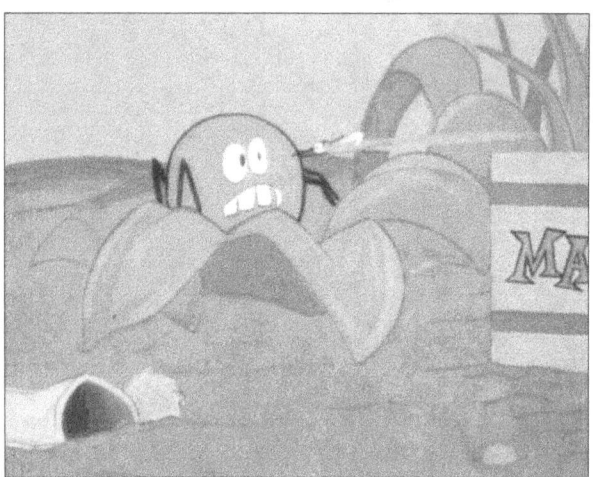

Fearless Fly in "The Spider Spiter"

In what is the second "Fearless Fly" adventure produced, Professor Weirdo, using a telescope, spies on Hiram Fly and his friends. He comes to the conclusion Hiram and Fearless Fly are one and the same. Weirdo creates a super spider to capture Fearless in a web. Fearless defeats the creature. then arrives at the Horror Hill castle to defeat Weirdo and Count Kook. This adventure was intended for "The Fearless Fly Show."

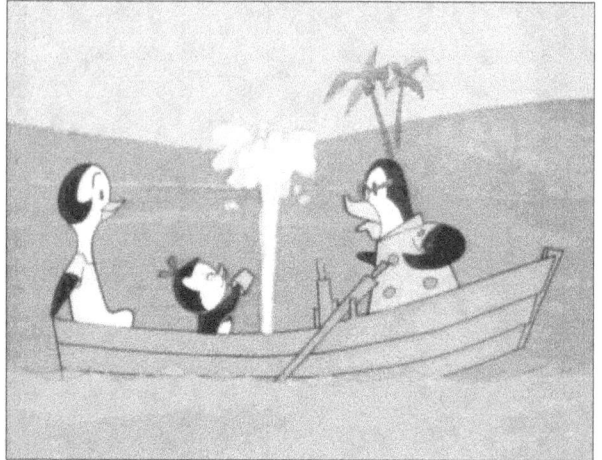

Penny Penguin in "Sickened Honeymoon"

Chester and Beulah Penguin embark on a second honeymoon and take daughter Penny along. Bad luck unfolds. Chester gets pulled over for speeding. The Penguins settle in their cabin. Penny goes outdoors and begins to disturb the other guests at the resort while chasing a frog. She drains the swimming pool, injuring her diving dad. On the lake, she pulls a cork plug sinking the boat in which she and her parents are riding.

34

Milton the Monster in "V is for Vampire"

A caped creature known as The Vampire has been leaving his signature "V" on the wall in Professor Weirdo's bedroom for several nights. Rattled, Weirdo is determined to learn the identity of the masked menace, so sets several traps to catch him. After all attempts fail, Weirdo suspects it is one of his monsters that is behind the visitations. He builds a secret trap that works, only to discover it is Count Kook who is the invader. Kook explains he was only trying to scare Weirdo out of his room because he wanted the bedroom for himself, since it has a better view of the cemetery.

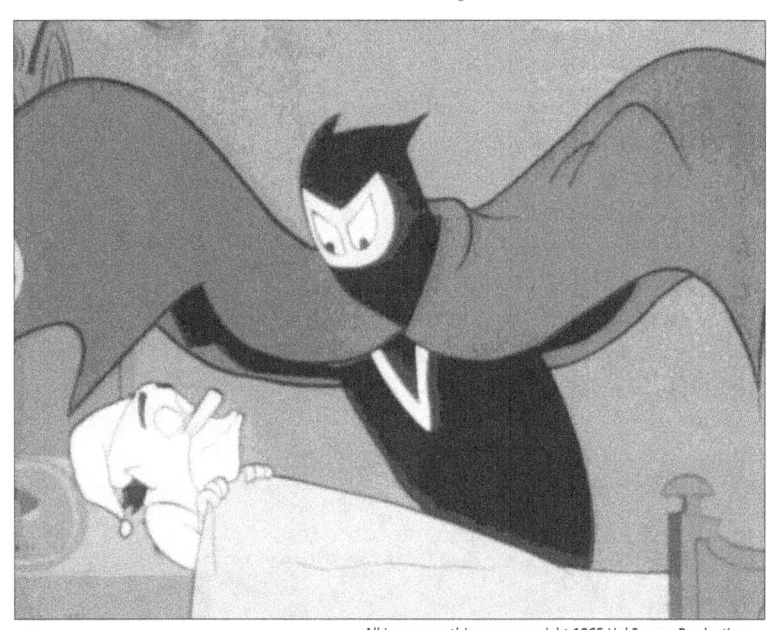

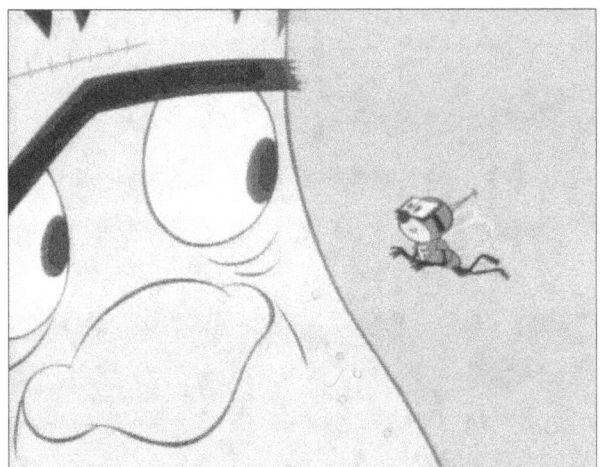

Fearless in "Fearless Fly Meets the Monsters"

In what is the third "Fearless Fly" adventure produced, Professor Weirdo creates a monster named George to destroy the hero. But Weirdo adds too much of the tenderness ingredient. In the city, the monster is kind and helps others. Weirdo dispatches his three other monsters to take out both Fearless and George, but they fail. This is the final of three pre-"Milton the Monster" productions intended for "The Fearless Fly Show."

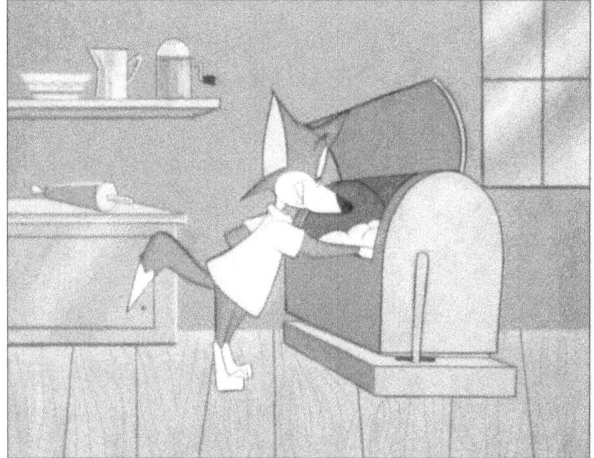

Muggy-Doo in "Crumb-Bumming"

Muggy-Doo stops by Osh's new bakery to wish him well. Muggy accidentally drops a silver dollar into a vat of dough and jumps in to get it. Encased in batter upon exit, Osh thinks it's an oversized talking Gingerbread boy. Muggy goes into the oven. Once out, he busts out of his shell. Osh tells Muggy he can have everything in his store if he departs and never returns. Muggy agrees, and finds his silver dollar, too!

Milton the Monster in "Monster vs. Mobster"

The monsters are playing hide and seek in the cemetery, when gangsters show up and bury a chest of jewelry in the graveyard. Milton sees them, and, knowing too much, is captured and taken hostage by the crooks. Heebie and Jeebie see the abduction and summon Professor Weirdo and Count Kook, who take the hearse to pursue the criminals. Catching them, the hoodlums agree to split the buried treasure with Professor Weirdo. Milton shows up in a police car with an officer and an old woman, who is the owner of the treasure. Weirdo is arrested as an accomplice and Milton receives a reward.

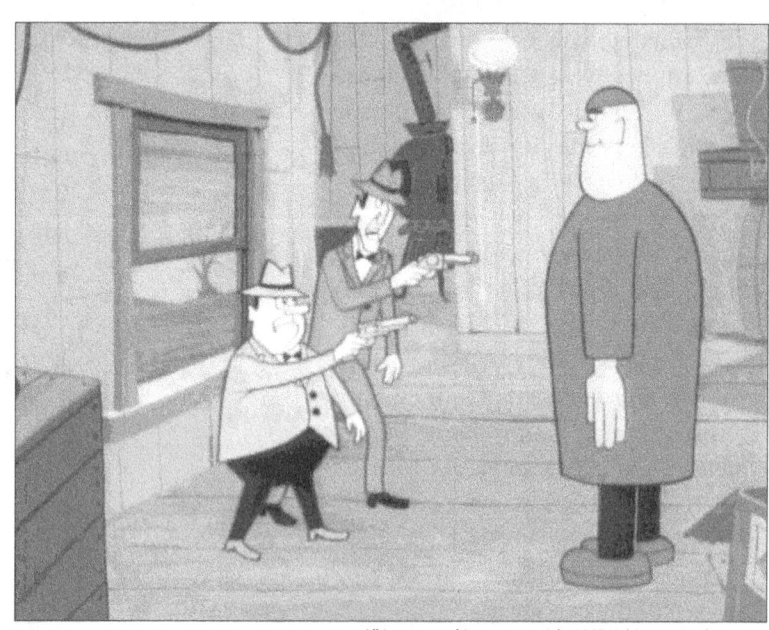

All images on this page copyright 1965 Hal Seeger Productions.

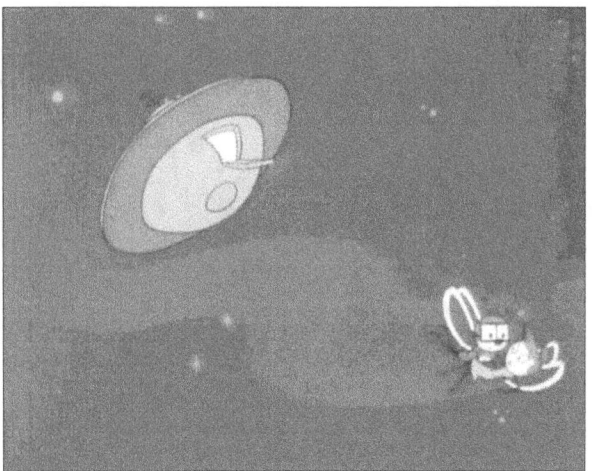

Fearless in "The Martians Meet their Match"

A flying saucer from Mars lands in a park in the middle of the city. Their mission is to find and capture Fearless Fly, to learn the secrets of his power. To attract the attention of Fearless Fly, the Martians create mayhem in the city, leaving a path of destruction to attract Fearless. The hero comes to the rescue. Unable to catch Fearless, the aliens abduct Flory. Fearless rescues her and tosses the saucer like a Frisbee, deep into space.

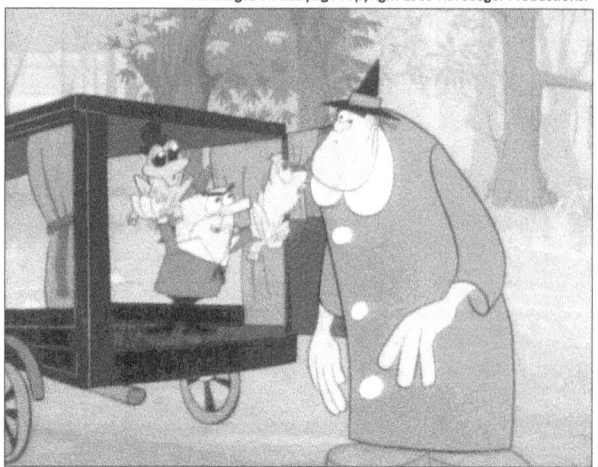

Milton the Monster in "Witch Crafty"

In a second Milton adventure in show #17, Milton stumbles upon a meeting of witches in the woods. Milton tells the others. Professor Weirdo sees it as an opportunity to spy on the group and learn their secrets of witchcraft. A witch changes Heebie and Jeebie into frogs. Weirdo dresses Milton as a witch and he joins the witches. They give him the Witch of the Year award. He's granted a wish, and Heebie and Jeebie return to normal.

Milton the Monster in "Camp Gitchy Gloomy"

Desiring peace and silence in the castle, Professor Weirdo takes Milton, Heebie, and Jeebie to Camp Gitchy Gloomy. The camp counselor, Harvey, is a tad creeped out by the trio, but does his best to teach his students the benefits of outdoor life. Harvey's taste buds are put to the test when the boys cook up some fat bat, candied crocodile, and spider cider. In a lesson in lifesaving on the lake, Harvey gets an anchor to the head. Milton learns craft-making and creates a mechanical man. Harvey is delighted when they leave, but Weirdo isn't, when the noisy gang return home.

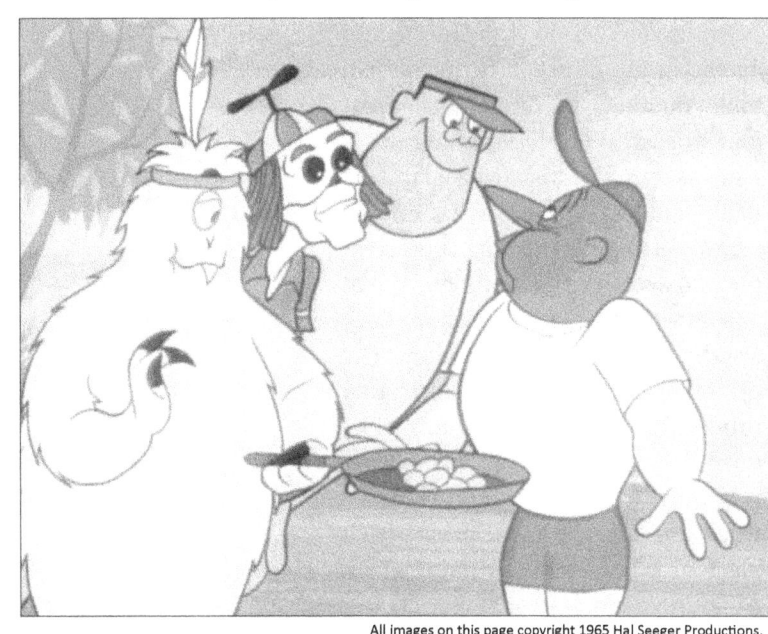

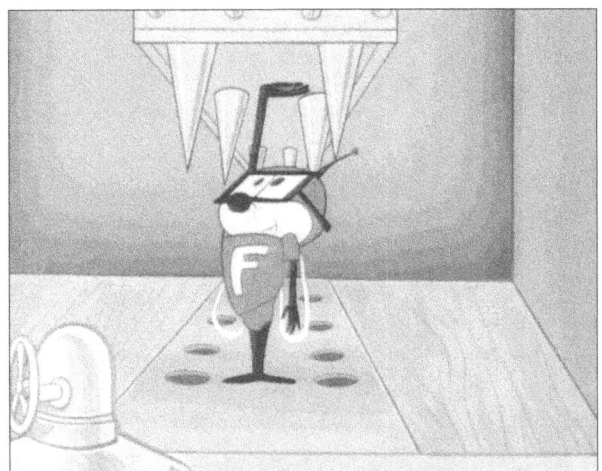

Fearless Fly in "Let's Phase It"

The president of World Wide Products installs a new computer system to cut labor costs. The programming of the new device is flawed, and the machines go haywire. Fearless Fly arrives at the World Wide factory, to gain control over the computer that is putting the plant workers in danger. Fearless discovers the punch cards were re-entered out-of-order, fixes the problem, and the plant is restored to normal operation.

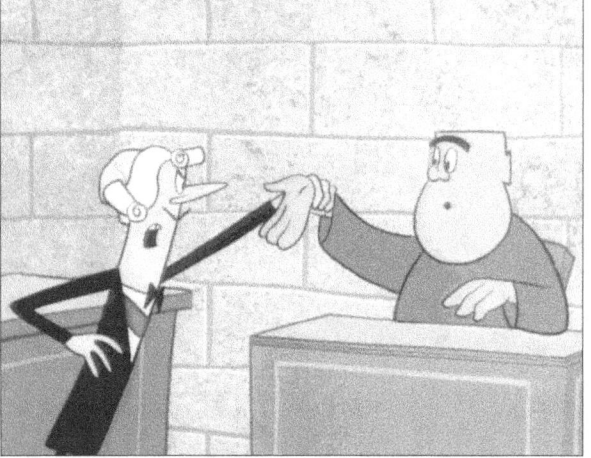

Milton the Monster in "Hearse Thief"

In a second Milton adventure in show #18, Professor Weirdo is alarmed when he sees his hearse drive away by itself. He, Count Kook, Heebie, and Jeebie go into the city to search for it. Milton, playing in the woods, finds the hearse and gets behind the wheel to drive it home. They think Milton is the thief and put him on trial. He is convicted and locked up. Milton breaks out and captures the actual thief, Professor Fruitcake.

Milton the Monster in "Boo to You"

Professor Weirdo puts Heebie and Jeebie in the dungeon for using bad table manners at dinner. The pair plot to scare Weirdo, dressing up as ghosts, but Milton overhears the plan and lets his maker in on the ruse. Weirdo plays along. Then Heebie and Jeebie run into a pair of real ghosts who navigate the castle. They are the spirits of their ancestors. The professor encounters the ghosts, and thinks they are Heebie and Jeebie, until they travel through walls, leaving him frightened. Milton intervenes and hits the apparitions with a blast of black smoke, driving them from the castle.

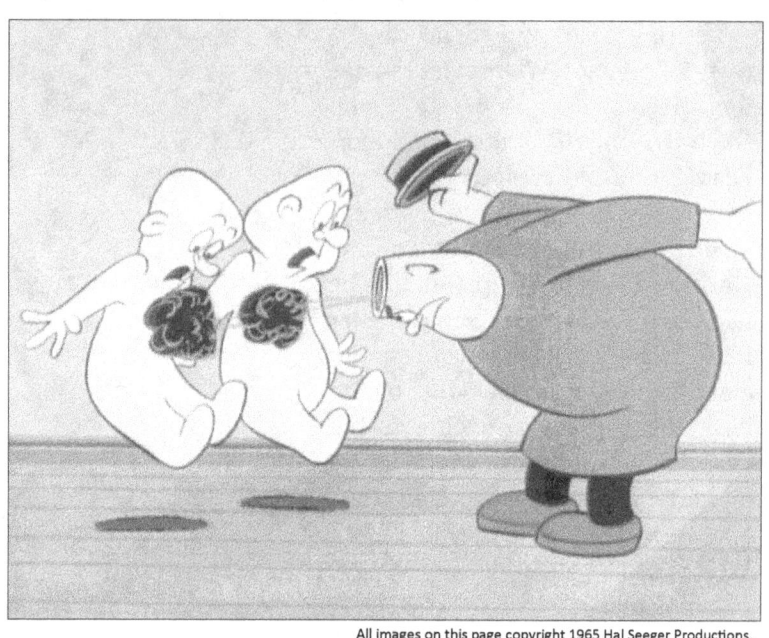

All images on this page copyright 1965 Hal Seeger Productions.

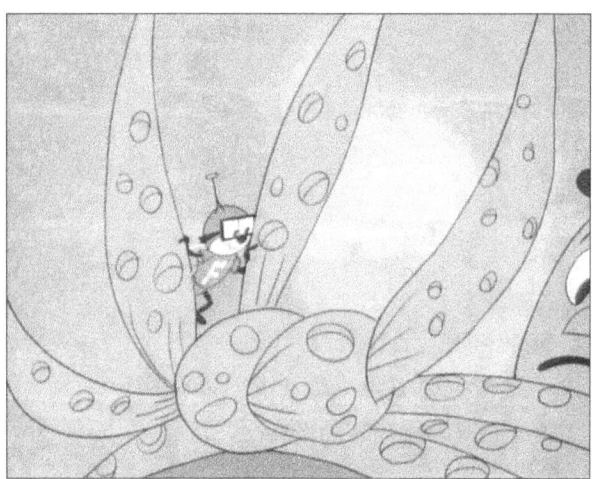

Fearless Fly in "Under Waterloo"

Hiram the Fly enjoys a day at the beach with Horsey and Flory. Offshore, beneath the ocean, is the city of Wetropolis. It is ruled by Barry Cuda, whose team includes Rock Octopus, Sparky Eel, and Ripper the Whale. Cuda plans to devour the land, turning it into an ocean. His giant clams take out several islands, then head to the coast. Hiram changes into Fearless Fly, defeats the clams and the whale, then polishes off Cuda.

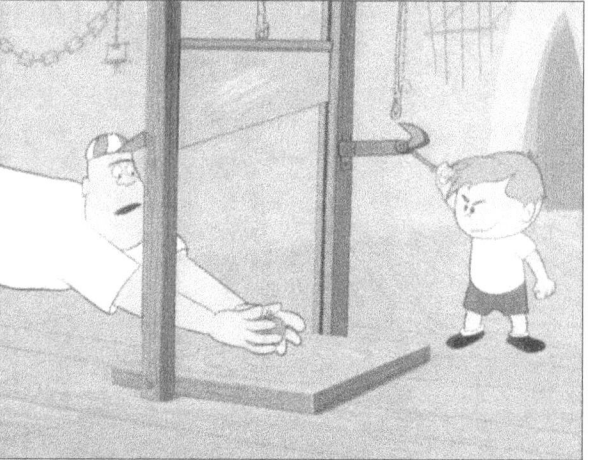

Milton the Monster in "Kid Stuff"

In a second Milton adventure in show #19, Professor Weirdo decides to adopt a needy child. An inspector from the adoption agency checks out Weirdo's dwelling to make sure it is a safe environment. They scare him off, and he accidentally leaves the kid, named Herbert, behind. Weirdo welcomes him in. The new addition turns out to be a brat, who terrorizes everyone. The inspector returns for the boy. They gladly hand him over.

Milton the Monster in "Horror Scope"

Professor Weirdo looks for signs of things to come using his horror-scope. When it predicts that another will become the head of Horror Hill, Weirdo intends to reverse the curse. He can do so by spending one hour inside a coffin buried in a grave. Milton assists, and later is knocked out when a flower pot lands on his head. The others are all alarmed because Milton is the only one who knows where Professor Weirdo is buried, and time is running out. An alligator burying a bone digs up the grave and Weirdo goes free. He returns to the castle to find Count Kook in charge and relieves him.

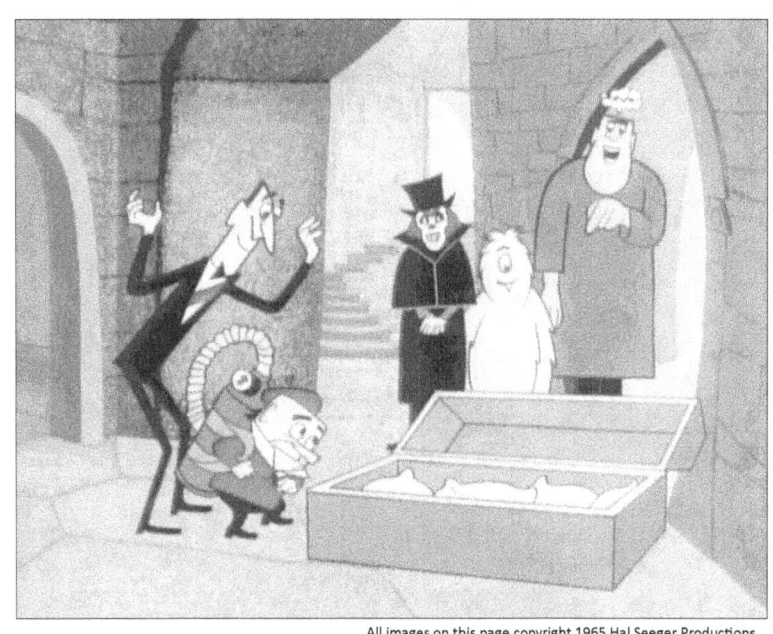

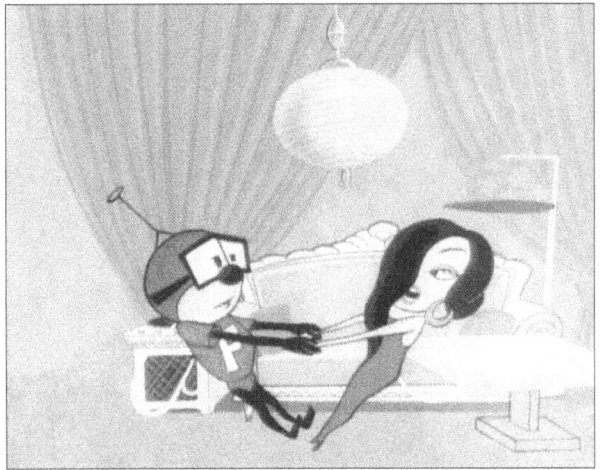

Fearless Fly in "Lady Deflylah"

Dr. Goo Fee and Gung Ho capture Hiram Fly and pressure him to reveal the secret of Fearless Fly's power. When this fails, they recruit beautiful Lady Deflylah to romance the secret from Fearless. The hero shows up at her love nest. She uses a mist from a perfume bottle, compelling him to reveal the truth. She takes his glasses. Goo Fee and Gung Ho place Fearless in peril, but Deflylah returns his spectacles, restoring his power.

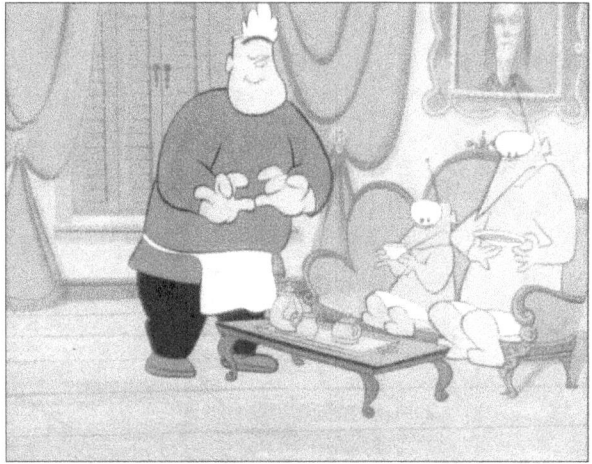

Milton in "The Flying Cup and Saucer"

In a second Milton adventure in show #20, a cup and flying saucer land on Horror Hill. Weirdo welcomes the pilots, two aliens, into his family, calling them "moonsters." The creatures begin eating everything in sight. Weirdo calls Fangenstein and Abercrombie the Zombie for help. The aliens send them running. Milton's tea time for the visitors sparks a feud. They knock each other out and are sent back into space.

Milton the Monster in "Monster-Sitter"

Professor Weirdo leaves Milton the Monster in the care of Mike the Mechanical Man, while he and Count Kook go to the movie theater. Mike has hiccups and Milton tries to adjust his settings to alleviate the problem. But when Milton presses the wrong button and the robot explodes, the monster rebuilds him into a multi-task computer console, with disastrous results. Mike is a modified version of the robot that appeared as one of Professor Weirdo's creations in "Fearless Fly Meets the Monsters," a pre-"Milton the Monster" production intended for "The Fearless Fly Show."

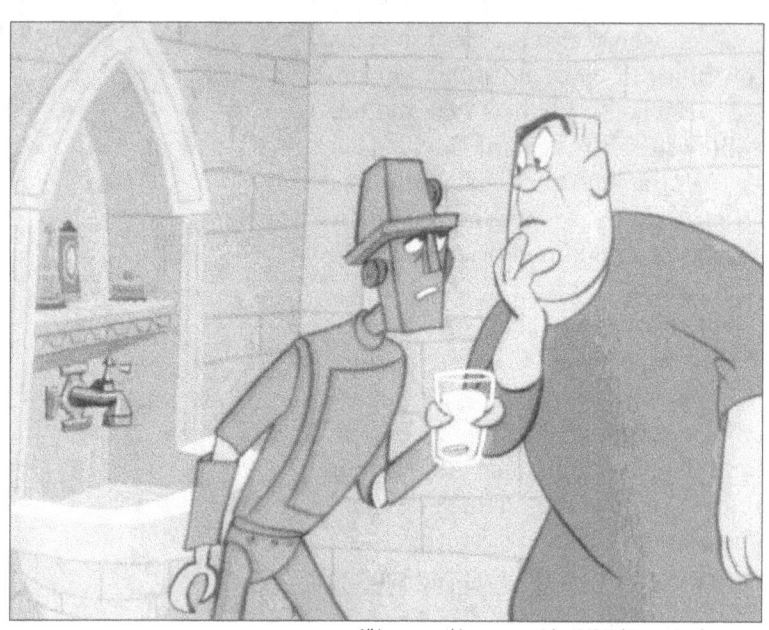

All images on this page copyright 1965 Hal Seeger Productions.

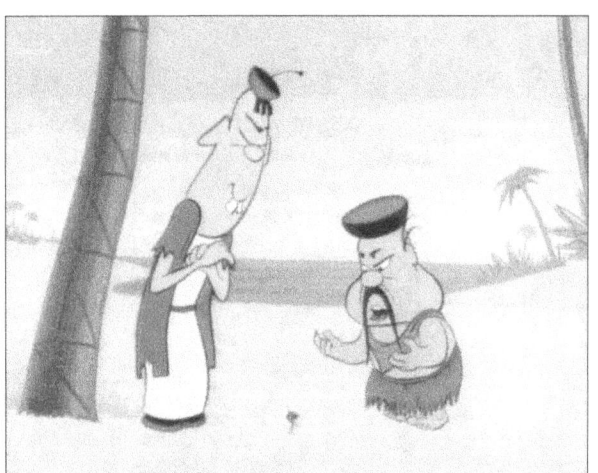

Fearless Fly in "Robinson Shoesole"

Dr. Goo Fee and Gung Ho are forced to bail out of their plane, taking refuge on a deserted island. Fearless Fly finds their location with his powerful glasses and offers to rescue the pair. But the island isn't deserted, and the party comes under spear attack. The perpetrator is Robinson Shoesole, who captures all three, to cook them for dinner. Fearless escapes and saves the day, transporting Goo Fee and Gung Ho back to Tibet.

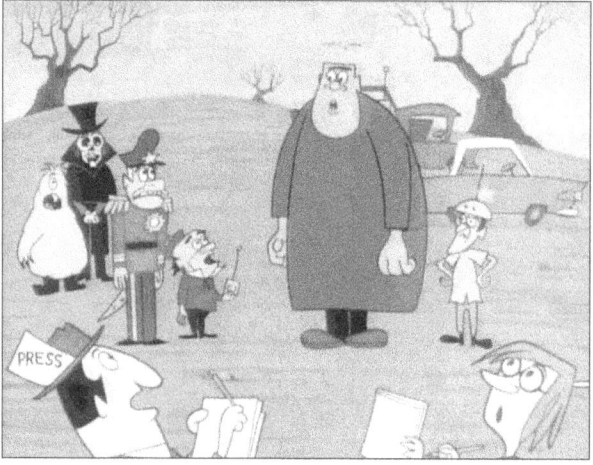

Milton the Monster in "The Moon Goons"

In a second Milton adventure in show #21, Professor Weirdo and Count Kook believe blasts from Milton's head could make him a rocket to land on the moon. Milton blasts off and makes a landing. Weirdo becomes a celebrity. But Milton has touched down a short distance from Horror Hill on earth. He runs into a TV reporter and the truth is revealed. Professor Weirdo is called a fake, but Milton gets invited to the White House.

Milton the Monster in "Think Shrink"

Heebie and Jeebie try to get the shrunken head to reveal where he buried the shrunken treasure. Fangenstein, on a motorcycle, steals the head, so he can acquire the answer. Heebie and Jebbie give chase, and recover the head, but lose it as it bounces off the hearse, landing among heads of cabbage in a vegetable stand. They recover the head again, but Milton snatches it away, saving his life. Grateful, the head tells Milton the treasure is in the cemetery. The gang unearths a barrel of shrinking solution. Heebie, Jeebie, and Fangenstein end up with tiny heads when they look inside.

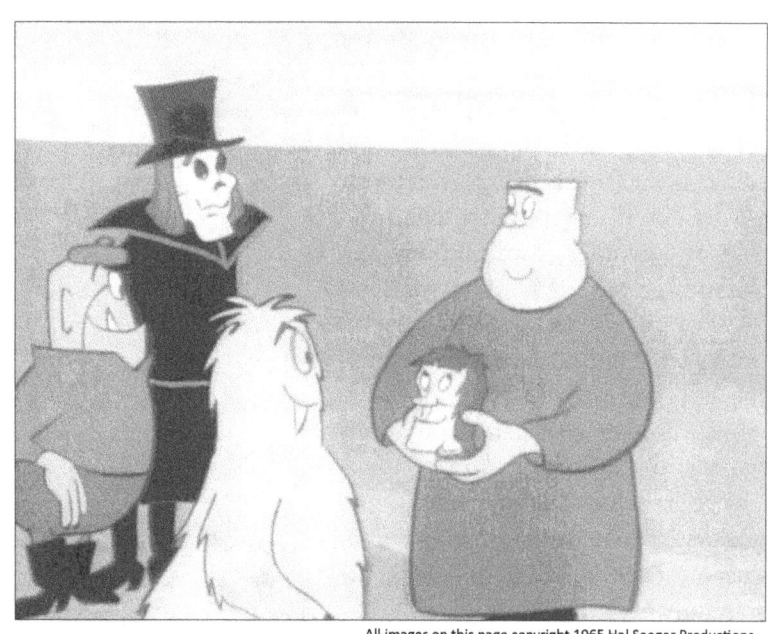

All images on this page copyright 1965 Hal Seeger Productions.

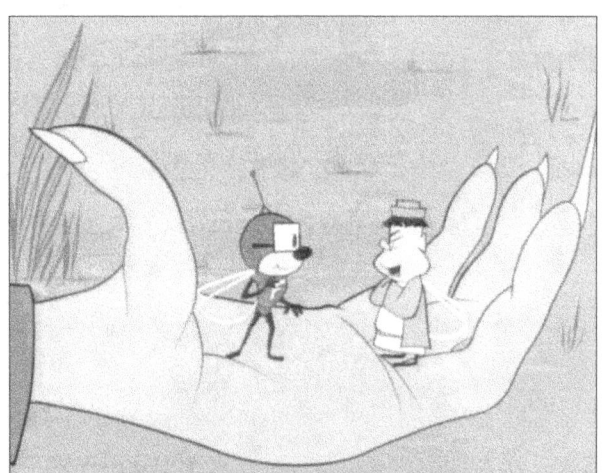

Fearless Fly in "Private Fly"

Dr. Goo Fee and Gung Ho arrive at the city dump to hire Private Fly, a detective, to find out the secret to Fearless Fly's power. Private Fly reveals his electronic computer brain can accomplish the task. Goo Fee and Gung Ho entice Fearless Fly to come to Tibet and see the computer. Fearless is tossed inside the device, but it yields no answer. Goo Fee and Gung Ho refuse to pay. Private Fly throws them into the machine.

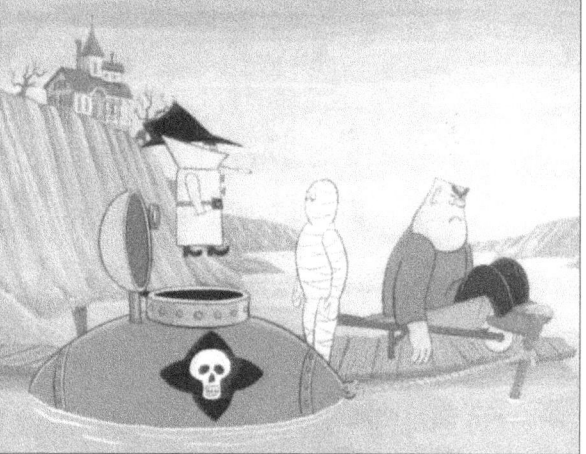

Milton the Monster in "Skullgaria Forever!"

In a second Milton adventure in show #22, Milton discovers a mummy hiding in a coffin at the castle. The visitor knocks Milton unconscious and takes him to a submarine, where an evil spy brainwashes the monster, compelling him to pledge allegiance to the nation of Skullgaria. Milton is sent to steal Professor Weirdo's secret formulas. Milton snaps out of it and breaks the spy's compass, so he can't navigate home.

Milton the Monster in "Crumby Mummy"

Everyone in the castle on Horror Hill is frightened when an electrical thunderstorm rages outside. A bolt of lightning enters the residence and strikes a coffin, bringing a mummy to life. But it's not just any mummy—it is an Egyptian guard mummy who knows karate. The mummy impresses Weirdo. He kicks Milton, Heebie and Jeebie out of the castle, because he is bored with them. Weirdo becomes concerned when the mummy goes into a destructive frenzy. Weirdo approaches Milton, Heebie, and Jeebie for help. Milton dons a suit of armor, enabling him to knock the mummy back into his box.

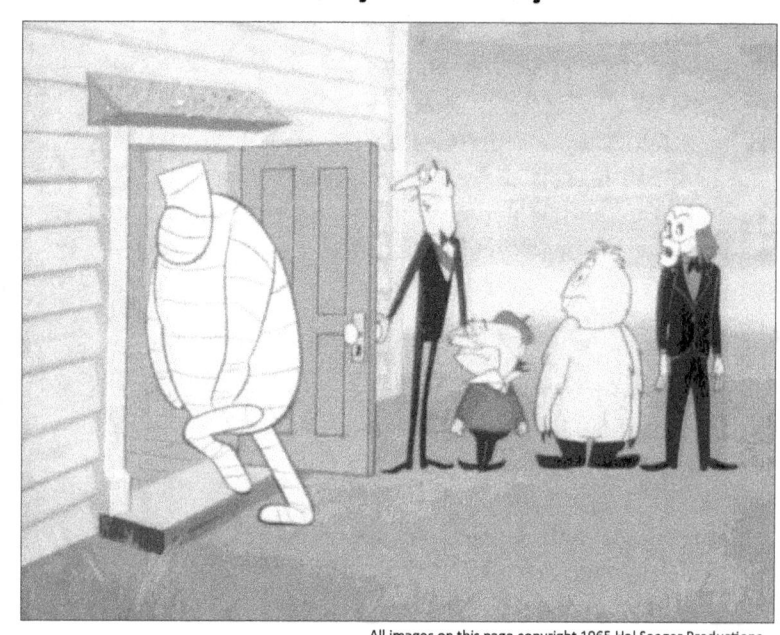

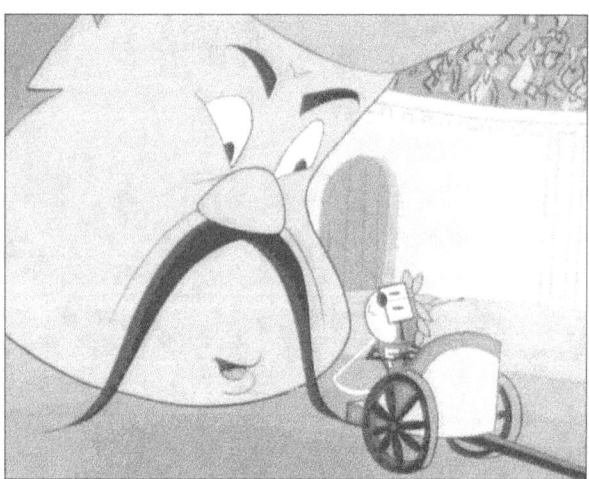

Fearless Fly in "Stage Plight"

Dr. Goo Fee and Gung Ho show up at Fearless Fly's matchbox, encouraging him to enter business. Fearless and the men head to Tibet to shoot a motion picture. Goo Fee stages dangerous scenes to eliminate the hero. Fearless survives the blowing up of a mine, a steer stampede, and a boulder dropping on him. Fearless' missing glasses are returned, to see to sign a contract. His power restored, it's curtains for the production.

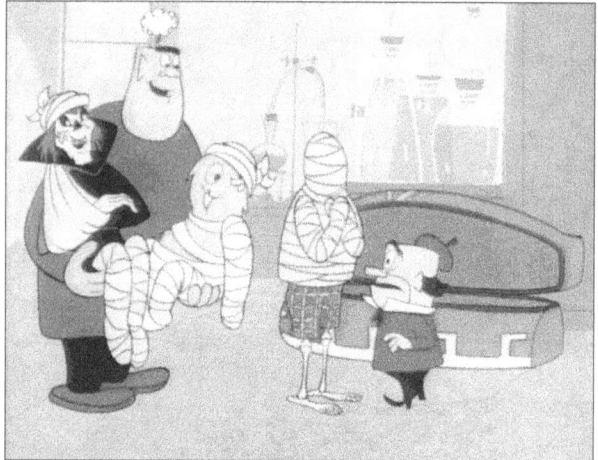

Milton the Monster in "Fort Fangenstein"

In a second Milton adventure in show #23, Fagenstein constructs a fort, and recruits Abercrombie the Zombie to help him capture Professor Weirdo's new mummy. Heebie and Jeebie join Fangenstein, and steal the mummy. Milton dresses as a mummy and is captured. Inside the fort, Milton ends the revolt, taking Heebie and Jeebie back. A showdown at the swamp between the parties ends with the return of Weirdo's mummy.

Milton the Monster in "Batnap"

Concerned Milton's bat, named Blackie, will win the annual Bat Derby, Professor Fruitcake bribes contest judge Fangenstein to help his bat see victory. This will be accomplished by a series of dirty tricks. They kidnap Milton's pet bat and replace it with a substitute, painted to resemble Blackie. It doesn't work, and Blackie is recovered. Next, they kidnap Milton and tie him up, as Blackie won't fly without his master's command. Milton breaks free, and the race is on. Fangenstein knocks Blackie unconscious, inches away from the finish line, but the bat manages to stumble across to win.

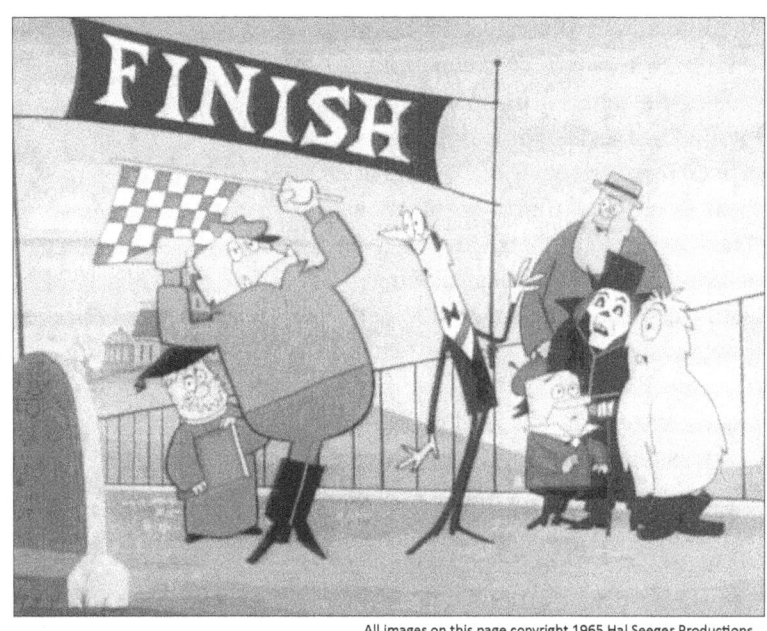

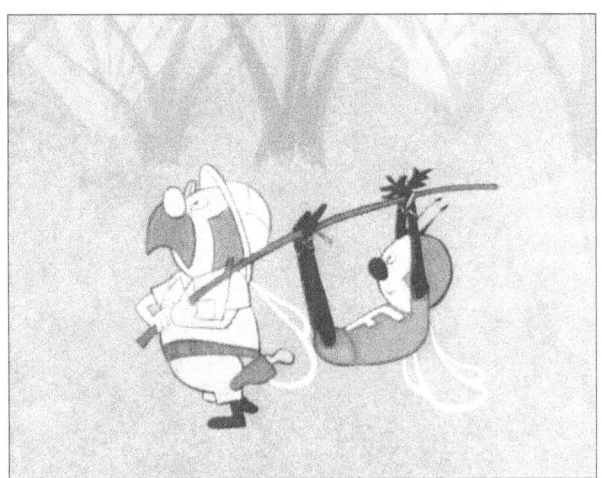

Fearless Fly in "Safari Harry"

Dr. Goo Fee and Gung Ho call for a truce and invite Fearless Fly to accompany them on an African safari. Setting up camp in the jungle, Goo Fee recruits Safari Harry to capture Fearless. Harry brings an elephant to use as a water cannon, but Fearless flees. The hunt is on. Harry catches the hero, but Fearless escapes. The drama ends when Fearless Fly dangles the elephant above his opponent's heads, resulting in surrender.

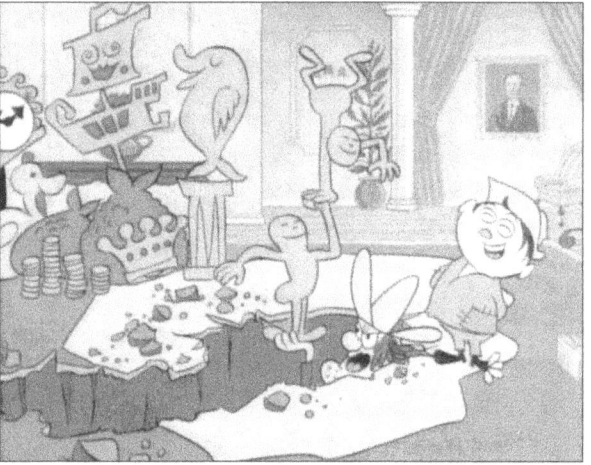

Stuffy Durma in "Nuggets to You"

Mr. Brinkley informs Stuffy Durma that 30,000 acres he'd purchased in Arizona, to build a housing project, has an obstacle. A man named Mr. Greedy owns 25 square feet inside Durma's land, that he must acquire, to begin construction. Durma strikes a deal by giving him gold digging rights on his property for the land. Greedy finds gold, but by digging into Durma's basement, where he keeps his precious metal valuables.

Milton the Monster in "Dunkin' Treasure"

Milton's pet alligator sees a sunken pirate treasure at the bottom of the castle moat. Fangenstein drops by and witnesses Professor Weirdo, Count Kook, Heebie, and Jeebie in a boat, dragging lines with hooks, looking for something. Milton carelessly reveals the secret. Fangenstein recruits Abercrombie the Zombie to help him find the chest. Dressed in scuba gear, the pair dive in. The race is on to see who can find the treasure first. Heebie and Jeebie descend in the water, wearing diving gear. The contest causes both sides to battle. But, the chest is found by the alligator, who reaps the reward.

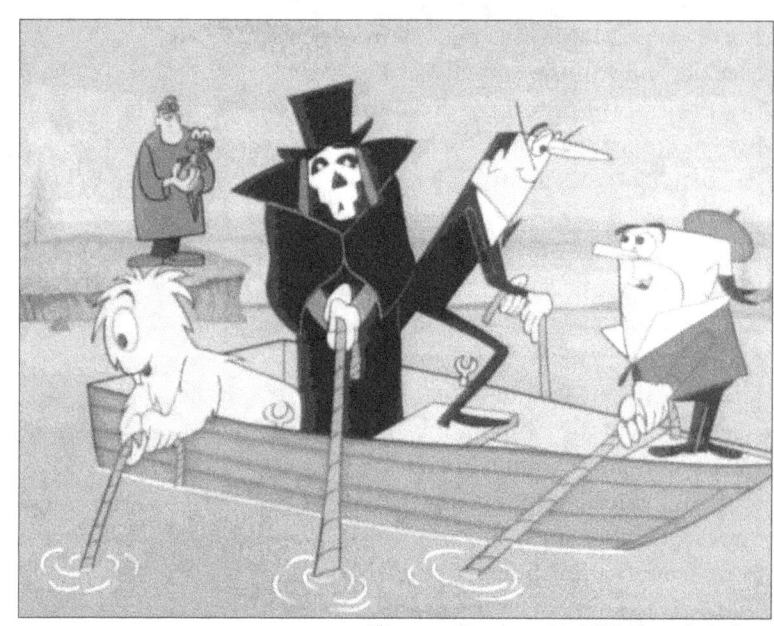

All images on this page copyright 1965 Hal Seeger Productions.

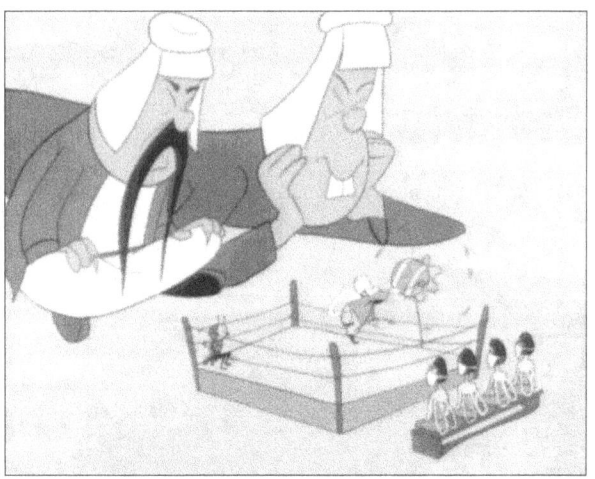

Fearless Fly in "Ferocious Fly"

Dr. Goo Fee orchestrates a boxing ring match showdown, between Fearless Fly and Ferocious Fly, at the Sultan's desert oasis campsite. Fearless seeks a victory in order to free his opponent's slaves. Losing his glasses, Fearless is at the mercy of the Sultan, who wins the first round. Fearless recovers his glasses and defeats Ferocious in the second. In one amusing moment of the tale, Fearless sees a mirage featuring Milton the Monster.

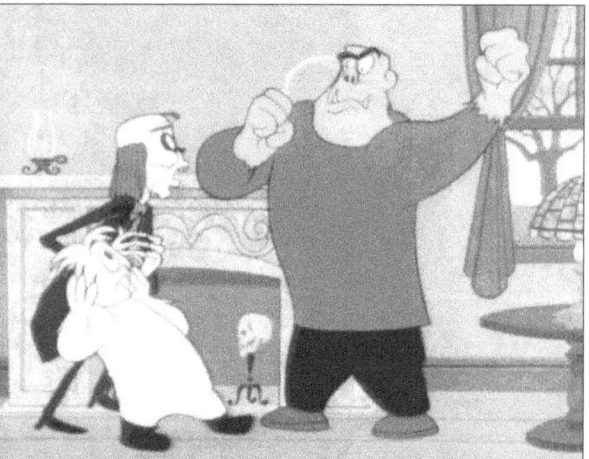

Milton in "Monstrous Monster"

In a second Milton adventure in show #25, the Mayor telephones Professor Weirdo, to inform him monsters on his property violate a city ordinance. He invites the Mayor to the castle, to see there is no threat, and the place is tidied up. When the party arrives, they witness Milton has turned into a beast, as a result of a spilled potion. The Mayor uses a tank to overpower Milton. A bump on the head restores Milton to his gentle self.

Milton the Monster in "The Mummy's Thumb"

Milton discovers a mummy's thumb inside the bucket in the well. Professor Weirdo is thrilled, as the good luck charm had gone missing. Anything the thumb touches turns to gold. Weirdo puts it in a safe and tells Count Kook and the monsters the item is to remain a secret. Milton, standing guard, blabs, and Fangenstein and Abercrombie the Zombie engage in trying to steal the thumb. All-out war transpires between the two parties' forts. Before both sides destroy the other, Milton releases a mummy from a coffin. The thumb is his, and he takes it back to do some hitch-hiking.

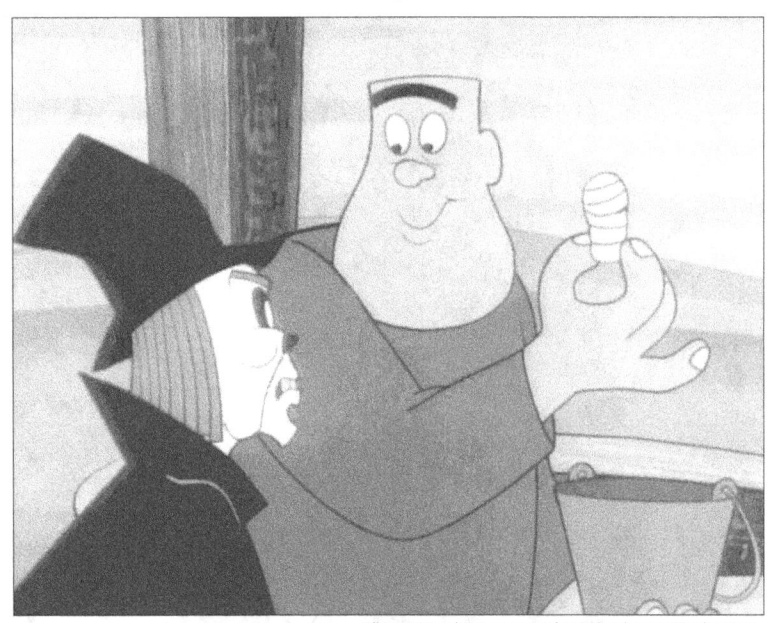

All images on this page copyright 1965 Hal Seeger Productions.

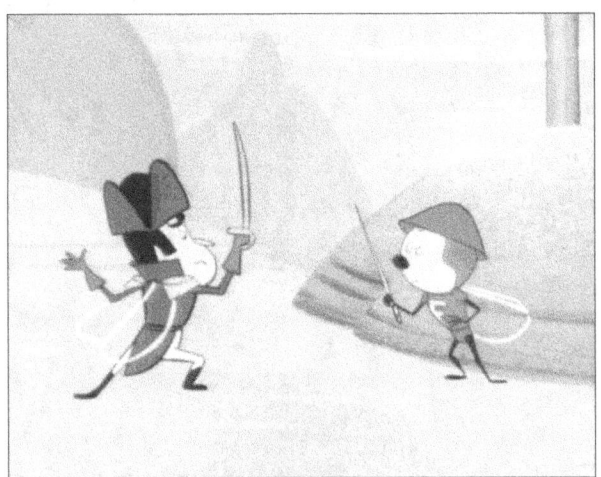

Fearless Fly in "Napoleon Bonafly"

Dr. Goo Fee riles soldier Napoleon Bonafly, telling him Fearless Fly has insulted him. Goo Fee then informs Fearless Fly that Napoleon Bonafly has declared war on him. Goo Fee and Gung Ho pledge to support Fearless as soldiers in the conflict. Fort Fearless Fly is established in Tibet, where the battle unfolds. Goo Fee and Gung Ho betray Fearless, who faces a firing squad. He repels the bullets and defeats his opponents.

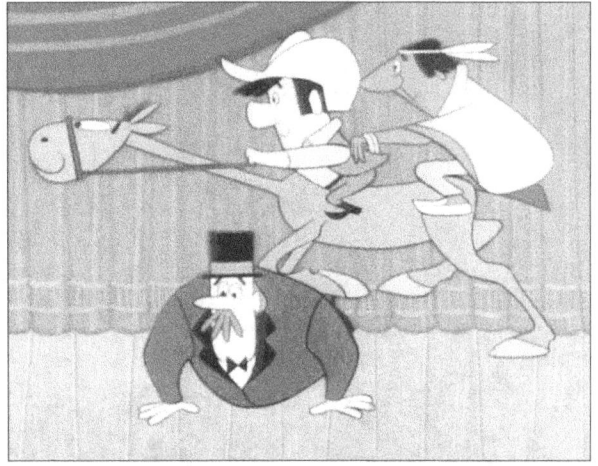

Flukey Luke in "Violin Violence"

World-famous violinist, Vladimir Loctoff, arrives in town. Novice musician, Rudolph Ravioli, dreams of owning a Stradivarius and plots to steal Loctoff's instrument. But he has to get past Flukey Luke, who is guarding it. Rudolph recruits his brother to help. The Stradivarius is stolen, and Flukey, Two Feathers, and Pronto give chase through the concert hall. They recover the violin moments before the maestro's concert.

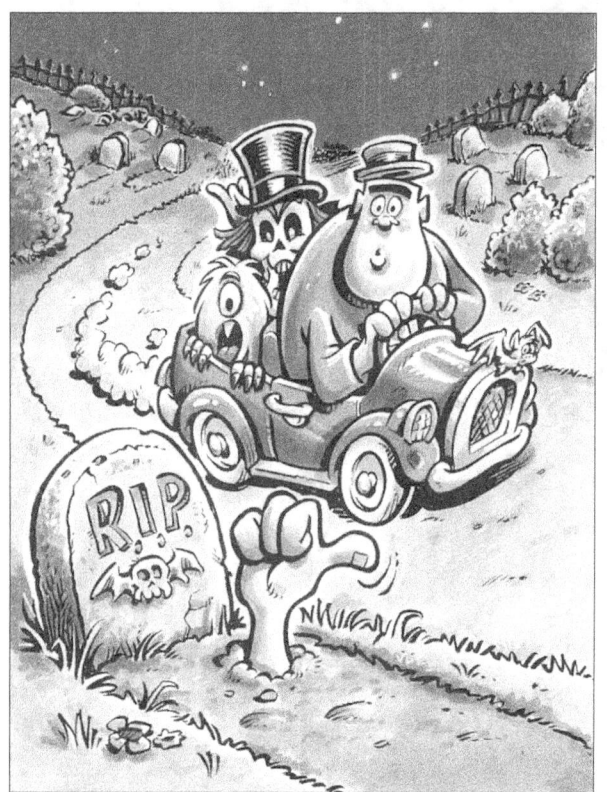
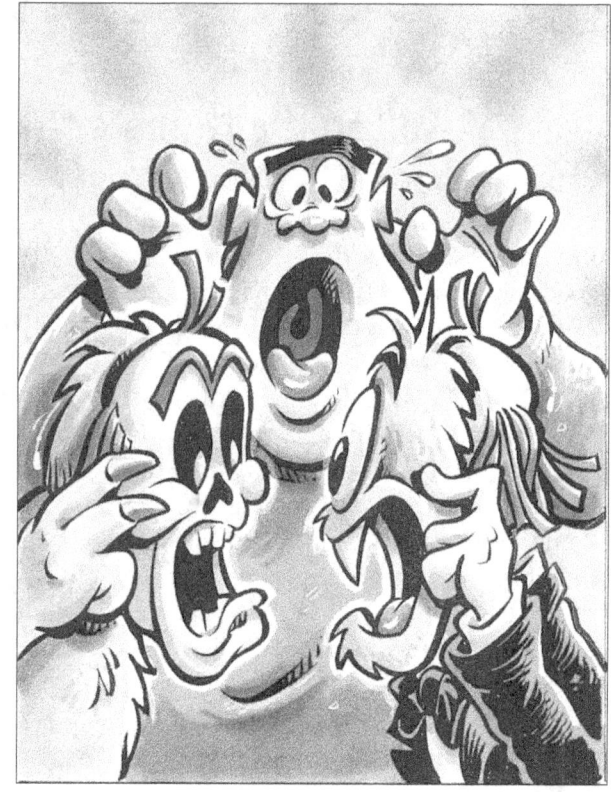
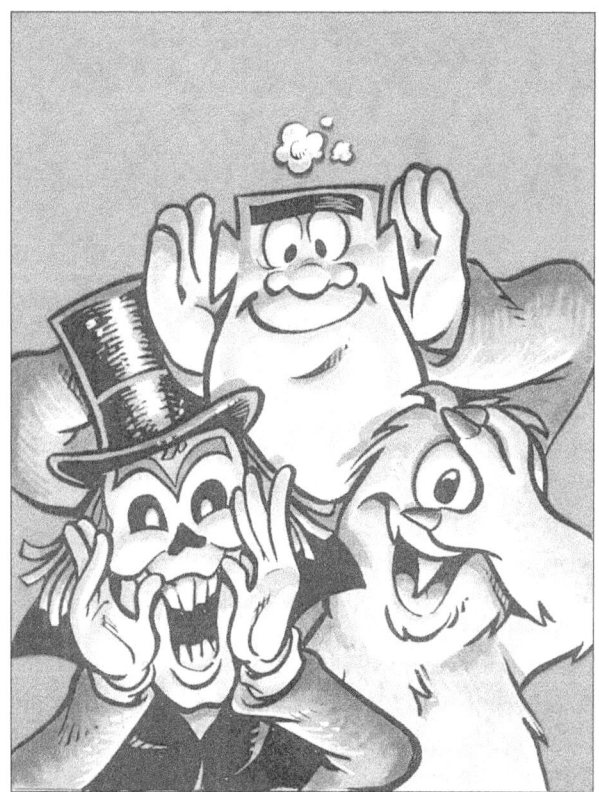
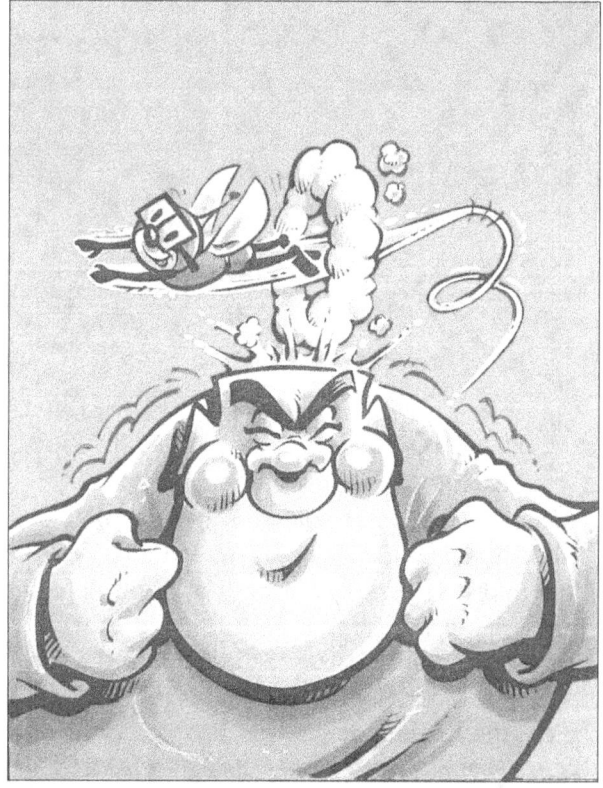

Jim Engel's cover artwork for four of eight Siren Entertainment VHS releases of the "Milton the Monster Show," 1999.

Milton's Resurrection on Home Video

The "Milton the Monster Show" last aired on ABC network television September 8, 1968. It would be over 30 years before the series surfaced again, on the video the home entertainment market. In 1999, Siren Entertainment, an Australian company, released eight volumes of the "Milton the Monster Show" on VHS videotape. Each tape included three half-hour shows.

Providing the colorful cover artwork for the tape volumes was Jim Engel, who was a Horror Hill fan from the start.

"I was nine years old in 1965, when 'Milton the Monster' debuted. As an aspiring cartoonist, and a Saturday morning cartoon addict, I became a fan immediately," Engel said. "There was a sort of strangeness, or weirdness to it, outside of its subject matter, that I couldn't put my finger on as a kid. As an adult, I'd attribute it to its New York origins."

Engel explained that the output of Hal Seeger Productions possessed a distinctively different feel from the California studios like Hanna-Barbera, in the same way that the old Fleischer and Terry studios in New York did from their Hollywood counterparts like Disney, Warner Bros, and MGM.

"The characters looked and moved differently, and the voices and humor were decidedly different," Engel said. "It just felt unlike everybody else's cartoons, and I think that aspect of Milton made it stand out from the plethora of cartoons available to a 60's kid like me, and it was definitely a highlight of my kid-hood cartoon fanaticism."

In 1997, when Jim Engel was getting familiar with the cyber world of the internet, a search for Milton caused him to stumble on a notice announced by Siren Entertainment.

"I saw a notice that a 'Siren Entertainment' had plans to release an 'Astro-Boy' on VHS," he explained. "I immediately emailed them, asking to be put on their mailing list, and almost as an afterthought, asked if they had an artist lined up to

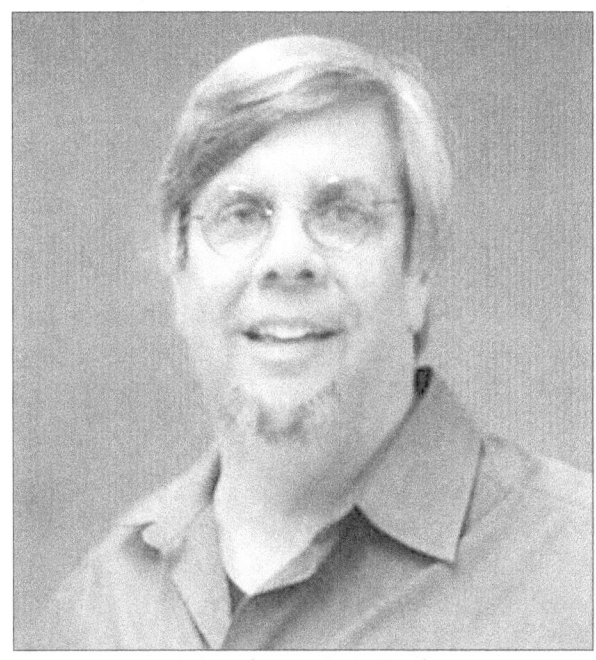

Artist and cartoonist Jim Engel.

do their video box art, citing my experience as a cartoonist who'd worked on virtually every major cartoon license in one capacity or another."

Engel heard back from Siren's Licensing and Distribution Manager almost immediately, and they were quite excited. Apparently, Hal Seeger Studios had nothing to offer in the way of artwork, and were going to rely on screen grabs.

"They asked, 'How quickly could you generate the artwork?,' adding that being only an Australian/New Zealand release, they had little budget. In fact, they had never commissioned artwork before," Engel said.

Siren initially planned a May 1998 release date.

"The internet made the world much more connected, and I'd had no idea when I contacted them that they were in New Zealand!" Engel said. "To make a long story short regarding the money part, they really didn't have any budget, or much time!"

Engel stated he completed the artwork for "literally 1/4 of a normal price I would be paid for something like that."

"I told them my main motive in inquiring in the first place was less a financial interest than a nostalgic/historic one," Engel added. "So, the small pay would not hinder my desire to do the job. As an old fan of the show, I just wanted to see it done right."

Engel produced 15 different rough sketches for cover art ideas, each one featuring a visual gag playing off the characters and monster/horror motif.

Siren selected 8 to proceed with.

"I then executed black brush line work for each, photocopied them onto marker-friendly paper stock, and did my final color art in design markers," Engel said.

Normally, Engel would work in watercolor dyes, but the tight timeframe and budgets called for the fast track results.

"Siren was quite delighted with the outcome, and I was quite happy to have been involved, and working on an old favorite," he said.

Engel never received complimentary copies of the tapes, but did receive the printed clamshell inserts for the first release (Vols. 1-4). He never got, or even saw, the remaining four in printed form.

Like the revival of Milton, Engel's artwork Siren has risen from the dead more than a few times.

"The art has lived on though, and is still turning up on DVD bootlegs—I see them frequently on eBay," Engel stated. "And as a postscript, when I saw the abysmal art Shout Factory intended for their complete series DVD box set, I immediately contacted them offering to do their box. Unfortunately, I was told they were just going to press with it, and even my offer to do it for FREE and within a week was politely declined. Oh well."

Shout Factory released their DVD of the complete series on March 20, 2007. The set has since gone out of production and is currently unavailable except at premium prices.

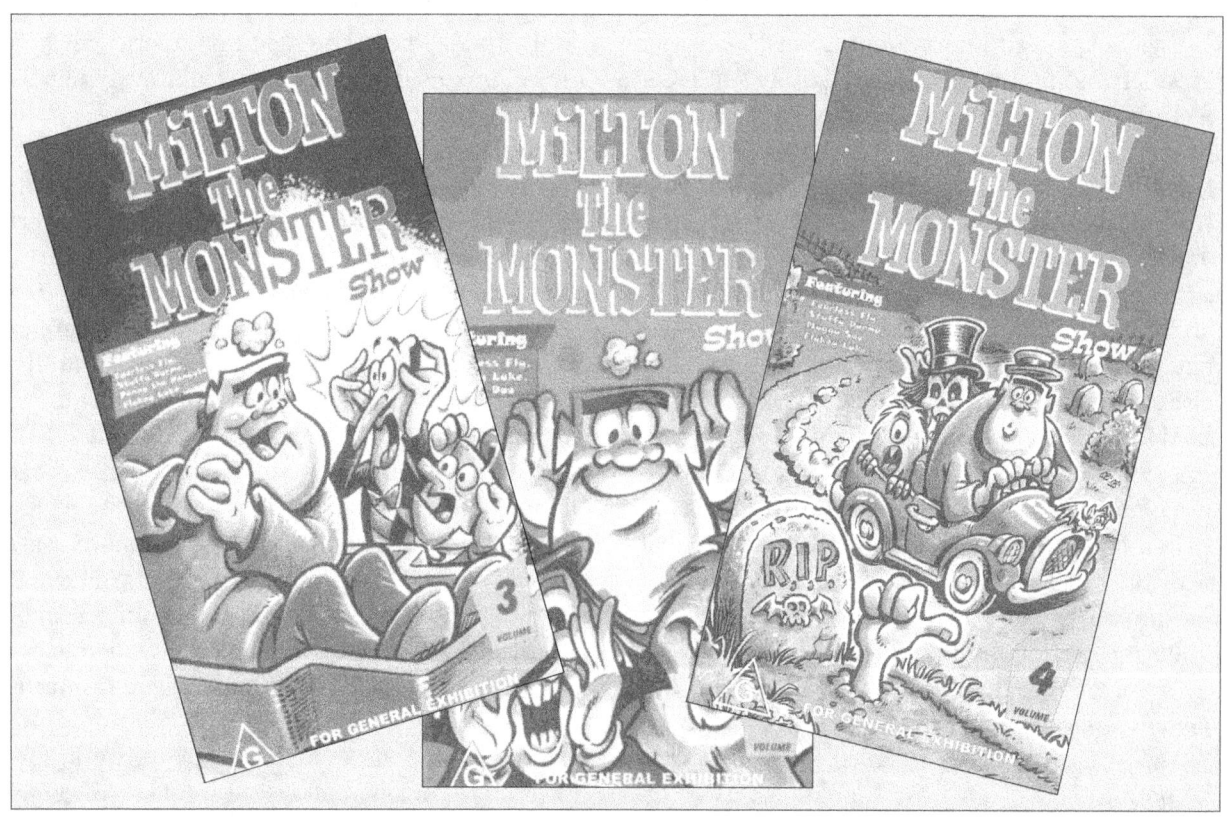

Three of the completed covers for Siren Entertainment's 1999 VHS releases of the "Milton the Monster Show."

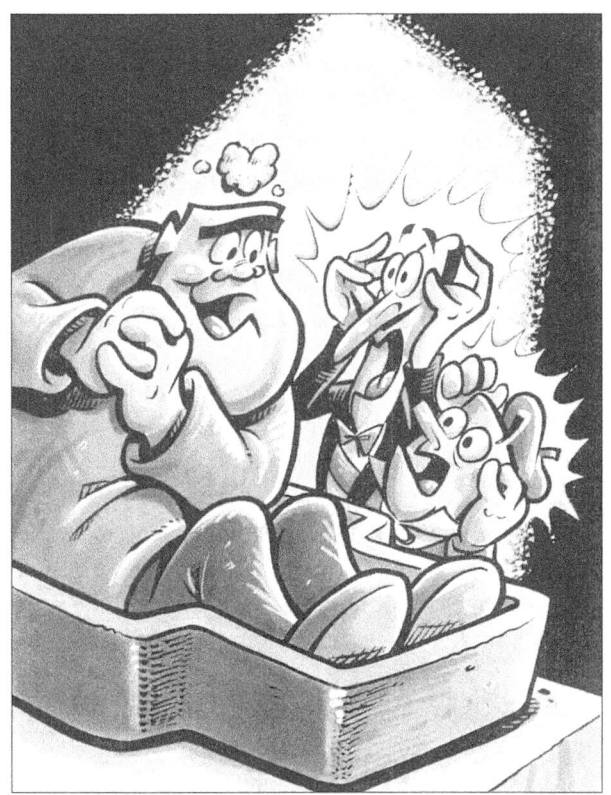
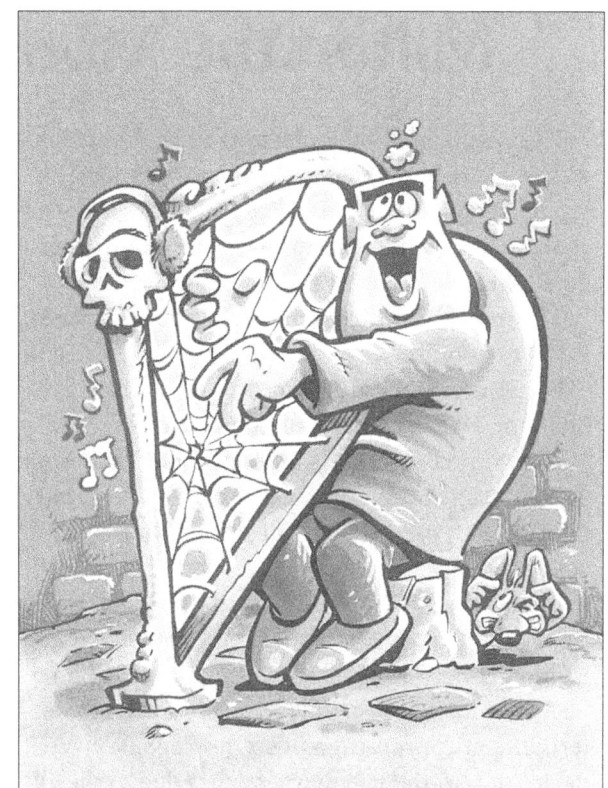
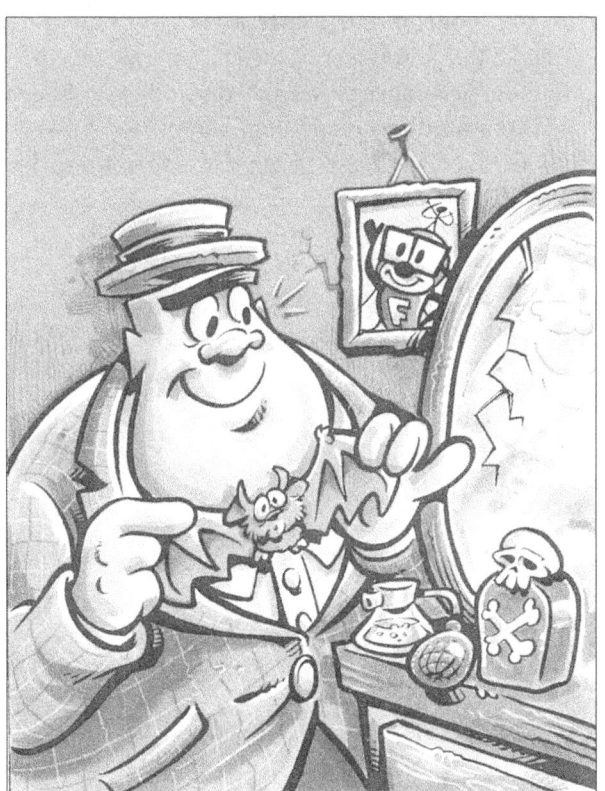
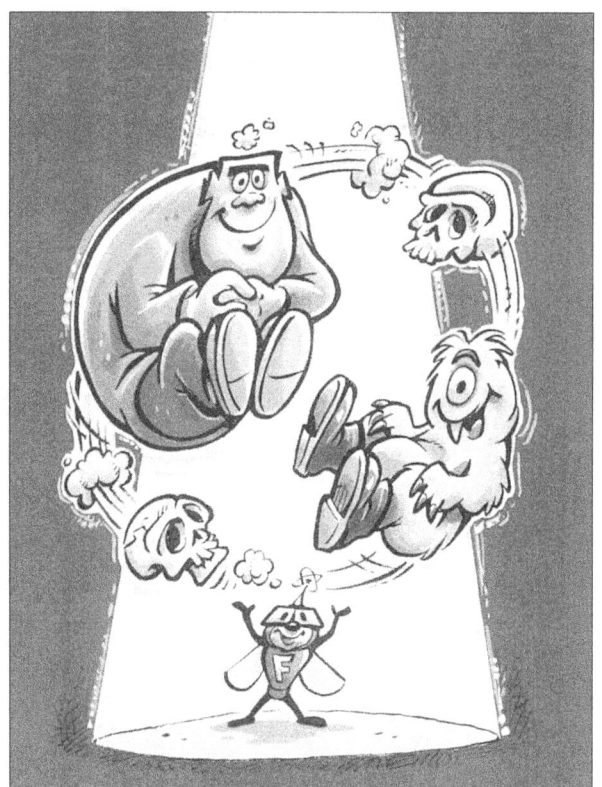

Jim Engel's cover artwork for four of eight Siren Entertainment VHS releases of the "Milton the Monster Show," 1999.

Milton the Monster Merchandise

Hal Seeger was fully engaged in the merchandising of Milton the Monster and Fearless Fly. When he attended the New York Toy Show in 1966, accompanying him were two individuals dressed in Milton and Fearless costumes.

The most collectible item of all, in recent times, is the cartoon series itself. The complete series of "The Milton the Monster Show," released by Shout on DVD in 2007, ceased production.

Amazon recently had an unopened "The Milton the Monster Show" Shout DVD priced at nearly $500. Good, used copies range from $99-$350 in collector markets.

As noted in the previous chapter, in 1999, Siren Entertainment, an Australian company, released eight volumes of "The Milton the Monster Show" on VHS videotape. While obsolete for home entertainment purposes, as very few people a VCR device to play them, a market exists due to the all-new original Milton the Monster and Horror Hill gang illustrations created for the box covers by artist Jim Engel.

Used videotapes of the series usually sell for $30 among collectors.

The majority of the merchandise tied to the Hal Seeger Productions cartoon featured Milton the Monster and his Horror Hill family.

Fearless Fly merchandise wasn't as typical as Milton. Fearless Fly usually was included in Milton the Monster merchandise, such as in coloring and comic books.

Fearless Fly items available were small and few in variety. One toy released was a Fearless Fly sliding squares puzzle, manufactured by the Roalex Toy Company of New York.

A player had to slide the squares around in the frame to assemble a picture of Fearless Fly. On the package, it noted that accomplishing the task in 10 minutes or less put you in the genius category.

Roalex also manufactured a Milton the Monster sliding squares puzzle, as well.

In 1967, Fleer released a small package of Milton the Monster and Fearless Fly gum that contained a tattoo transfer of the characters. Recently an unopened package was listed on eBay for $20.

Milton and his creepy family appeared on several cardboard jigsaw puzzles, manufactured by

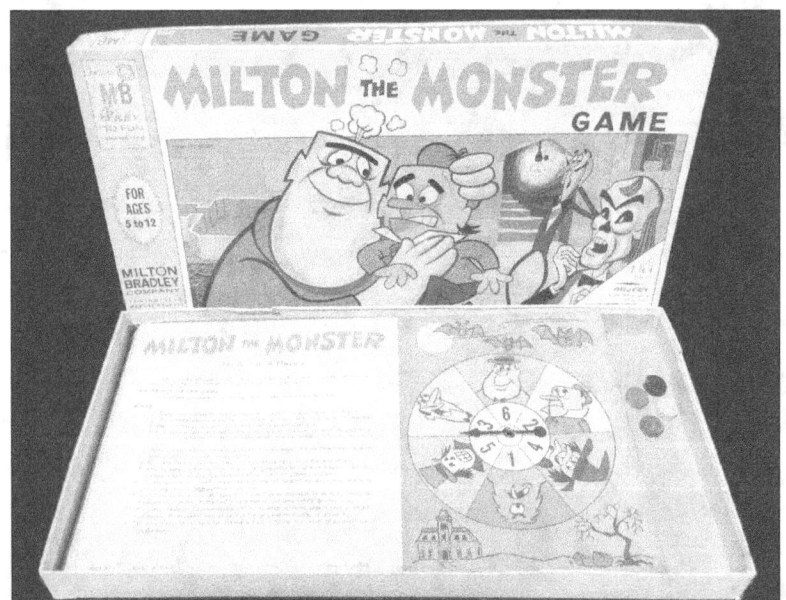
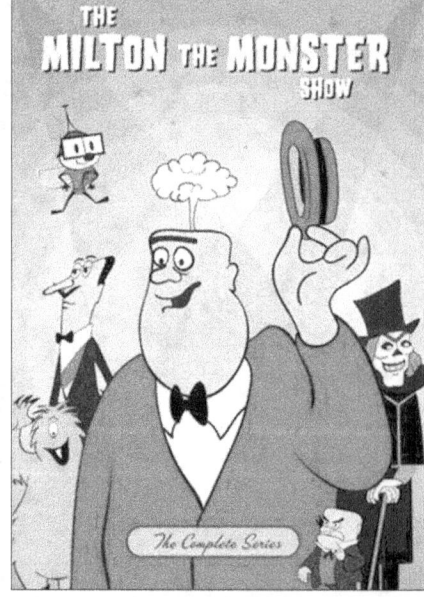

Left, Milton Bradley board game box, right, complete series DVD released by Shout in 2007, right. *Copyright 1965 Hal Seeger Productions.*

Whitman, who also published the coloring books.

One 100-piece jigsaw puzzle, released by Whitman in 1966, featured a picture of Milton the Monster in a classroom of students. One of the students is Professor Weirdo. It measured 14 x 18 inches.

Another Whitman Milton the Monster jigsaw puzzle, released in 1966, was a frame-tray puzzle, which provided a display container for the pieces.

Whitman Publishing released one coloring book in 1966. The edition, running 128 pages, featured the Horror Hill gang from "The Milton the Monster Show." The artwork was created by Jason Studios of New York, which provided artwork for most of the Whitman coloring books at the time. Pages in the book feature captions or descriptions relating to what is depicted. Many new characters, creatures, and additions not seen in the animated

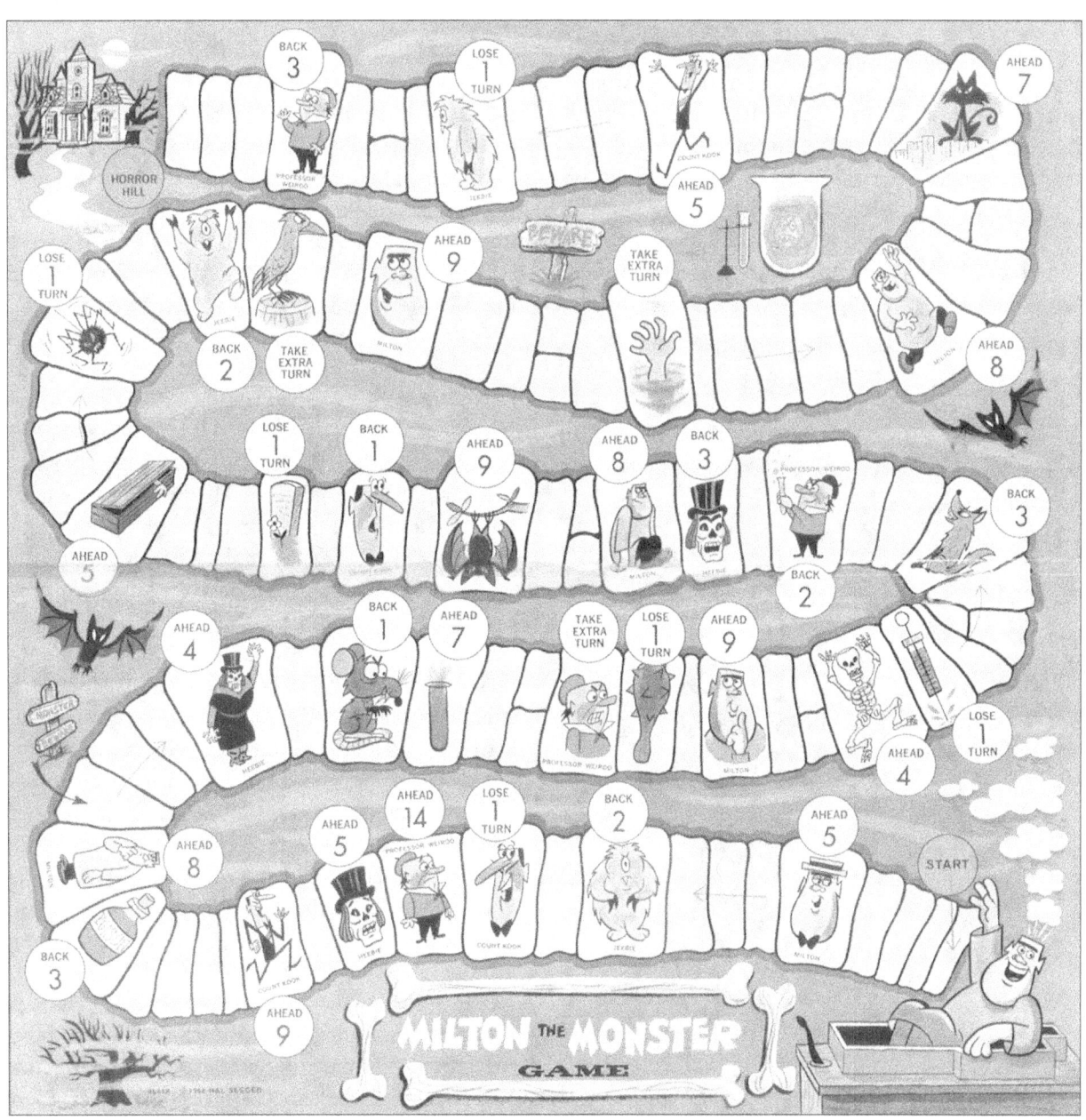

Milton Bradley's "Milton the Monster" board game. *Copyright 1965 Hal Seeger Productions.*

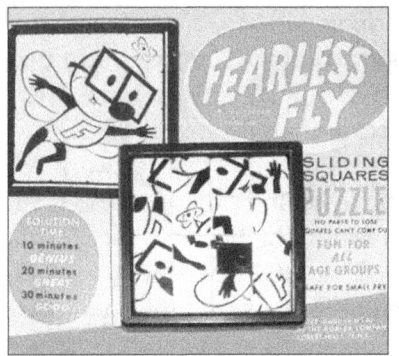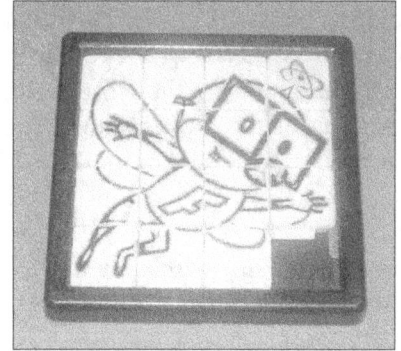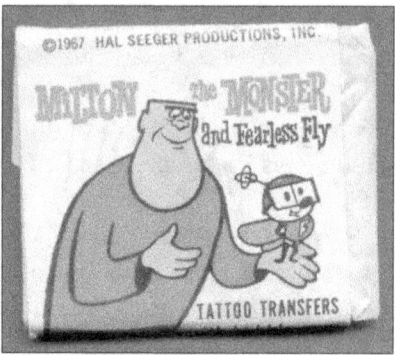

Fearless Fly slide puzzle and Milton the Monster and Fearless Fly gum and tattoo transfers. *Copyright 1965 Hal Seeger Productions.*

series appear add to the book's appeal making it attractive to collectors. An unused copy in high condition can fetch over $200 from diehard collectors, whereas books colored in, or in lower grade shape, can sell for under $30.

Gold Key published a "Milton the Monster and Fearless Fly" comic book in May 1966. The one-shot book, #1, ran 32 pages, with a cover price of

12 cents. While some themes in the book were taken from the television series, some new characters appear, such as a werewolf, that Milton befriends. The comic, among collectors, sells for under $50 in good condition, but 9.0 or near-mint copies can command a price of $150-$250.

Another comic book loosely related to Milton the Monster is "3-D Dell" #3, published in 1953, which features the original Flukey Luke dog character. The book came with a pair of 3-D cardboard frame glasses, sporting red and green foil lenses.

Milton Bradley released a Milton the Monster board game that sold relatively well. Players started their journey to Horror Hill with an image of Milton in his laboratory mold. Spinning an arrow on a dial, featuring numbers and faces of the characters, indicated how many spaces a player could advance. Besides depictions of the characters, the walkway to the castle featured images such as a spider, coffin, a black cat, a tombstone, a wolf, a skeleton, a bottle of poison and more. Some spaces were also marked with instructions, such as moving ahead, or behind, a number of spaces, or losing or gaining a turn to spin. The game could accommodate up to four players.

Not all Milton the Monster and Fearless Fly merchandise is from the time the program was originally broadcast. Redbubble sells newly designed t-shirts and apparel featuring the characters. Some feature new illustrations, while others reproduce familiar 1966 art, such as using the Milton and Professor Weirdo color illustration from the cover of the Gold Key comic book.

Gold Key Comics' "Milton the Monster and Fearless Fly" #1. *Copyright 1965 Hal Seeger Productions.*

Original animation art occasionally appears online, or at auction houses, for sale. Prices fluctuate according to detail and subject matter of an illustration or animation cell is and its condition. Other artwork seen in recent times available included illustrations from comic books and coloring books, as well as color paintings used for puzzles.

Fan art of Milton the Monster and his Horror Hill gang also appears on the internet, sometimes for sale, but usually created as a tribute to the series.

Milton and Fearless Fly t-shirts can be found online, but apparently are unlicensed products.

For a while, several episodes of "The Milton the Monster Show" were available for viewing from Amazon video. They are currently unavailable. Foothill Entertainment features a handful of Milton cartoons available for viewing on their "Retroville" YouTube channel.

Until the series is reissued on DVD, it appears the cemetery on Horror Hill will remain quiet.

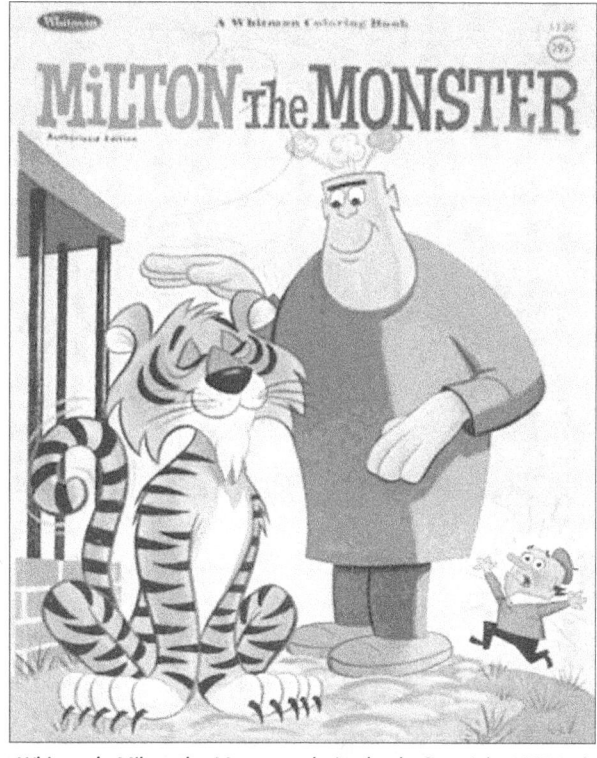

Whitman's Milton the Monster coloring book. *Copyright 1965 Hal Seeger Productions.*

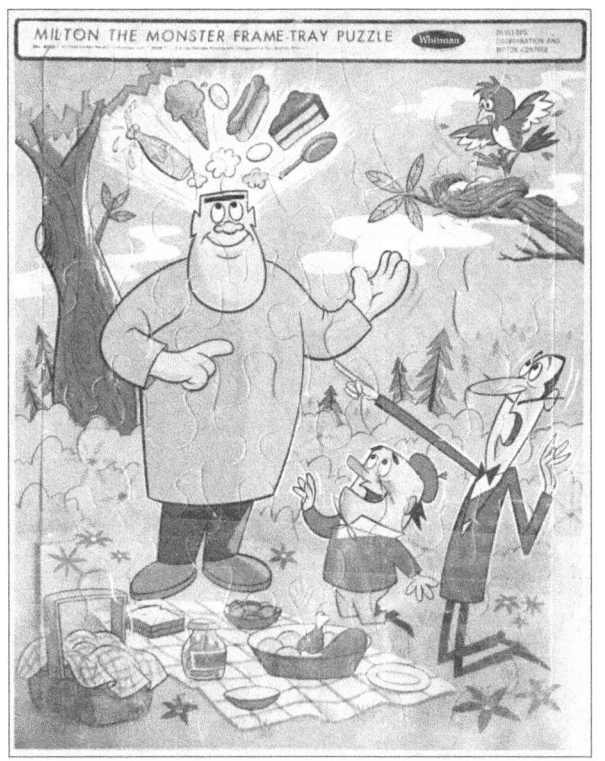

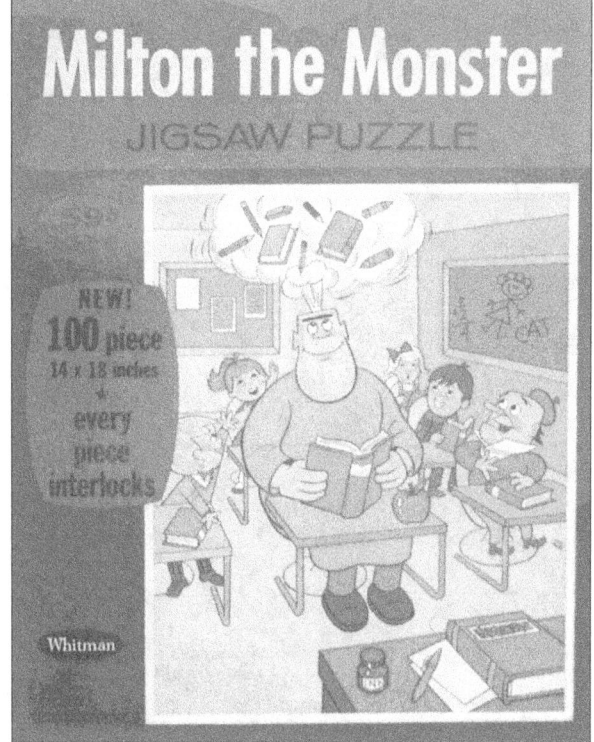

Above, Milton the Monster frame-tray puzzle and jigsaw puzzle. *Copyright 1965 Hal Seeger Productions.*

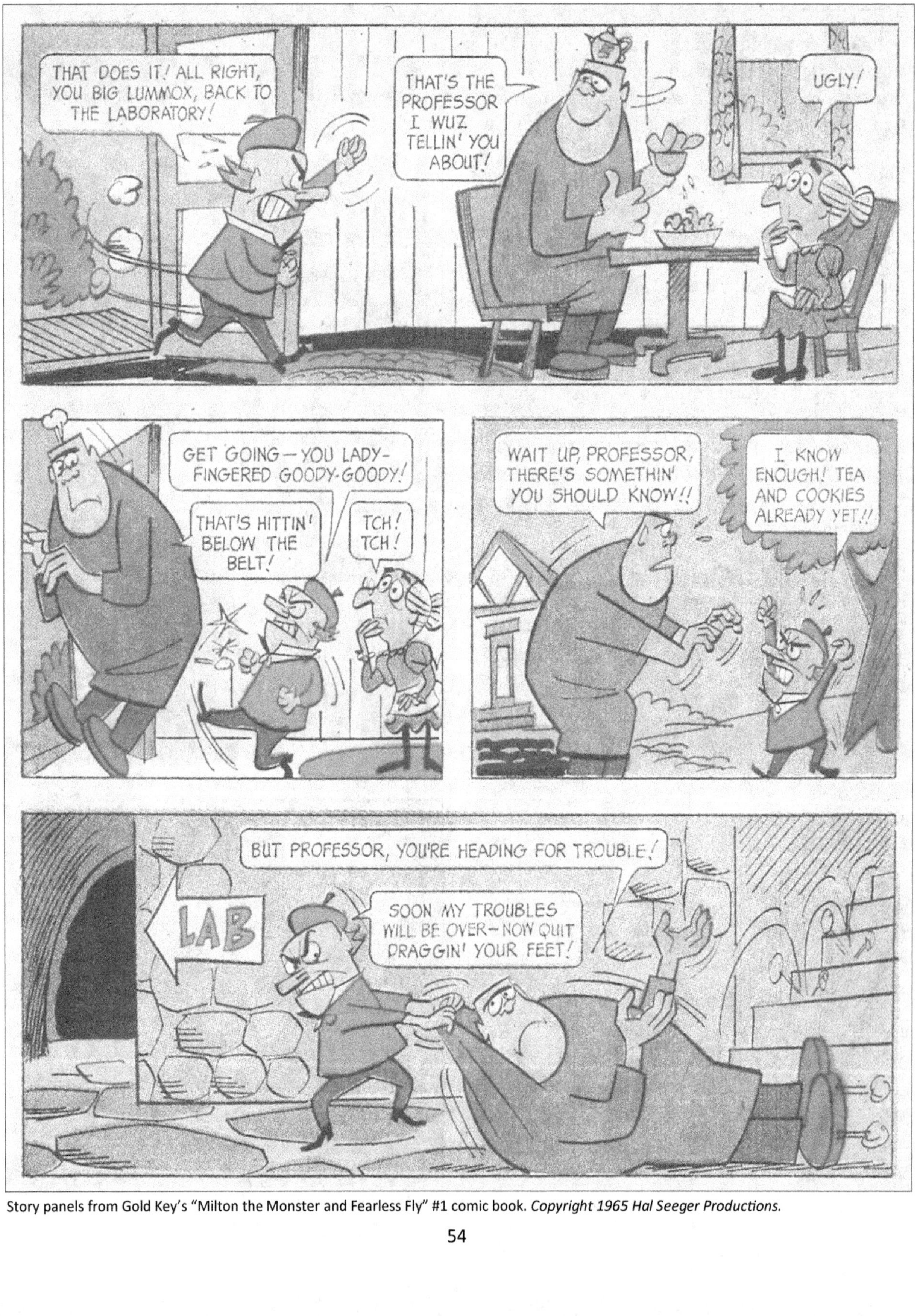

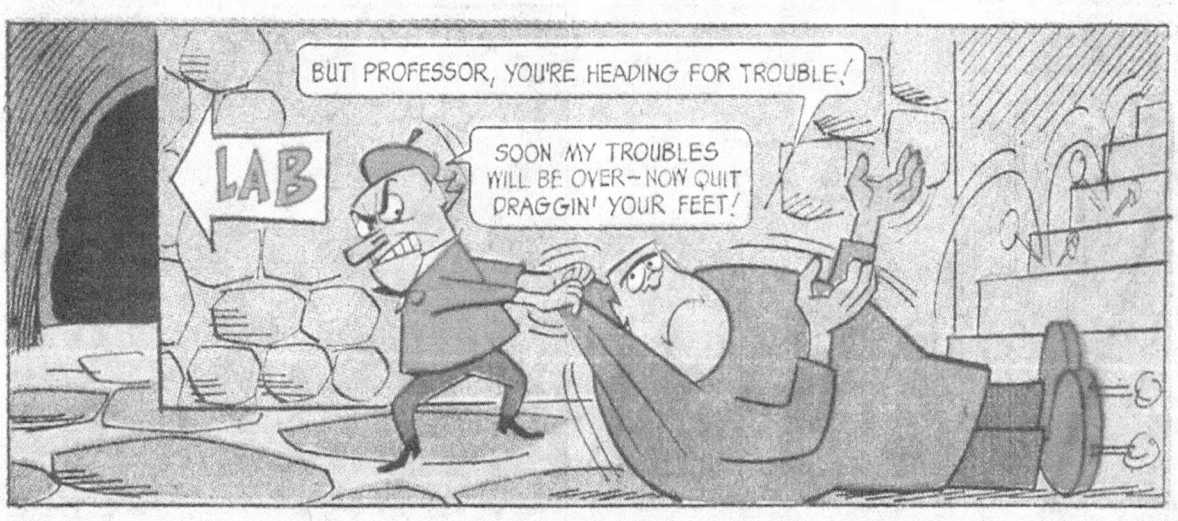

Story panels from Gold Key's "Milton the Monster and Fearless Fly" #1 comic book. *Copyright 1965 Hal Seeger Productions.*

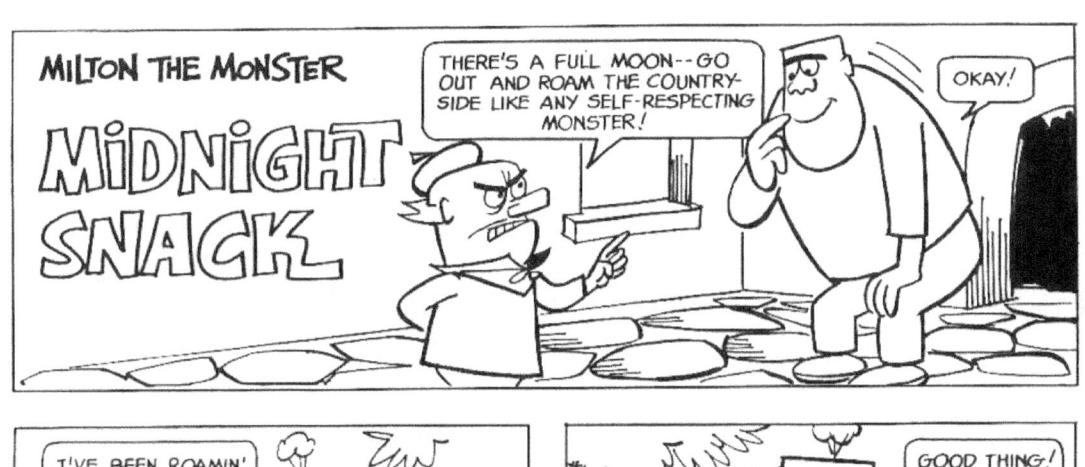

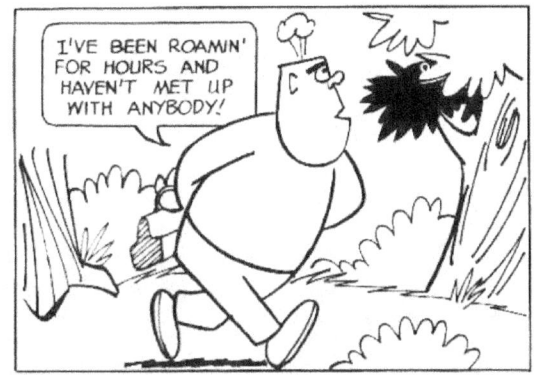

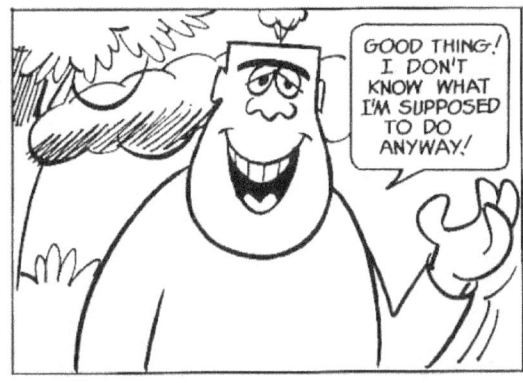

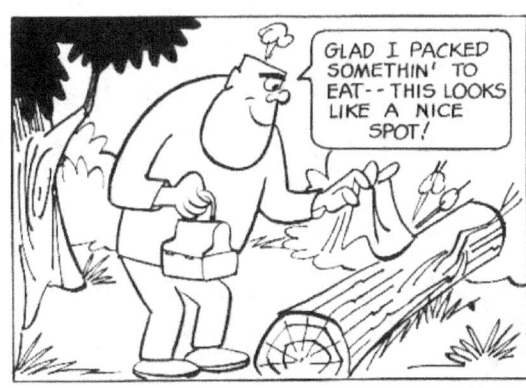

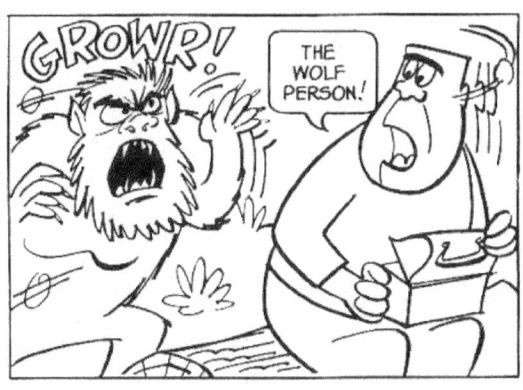

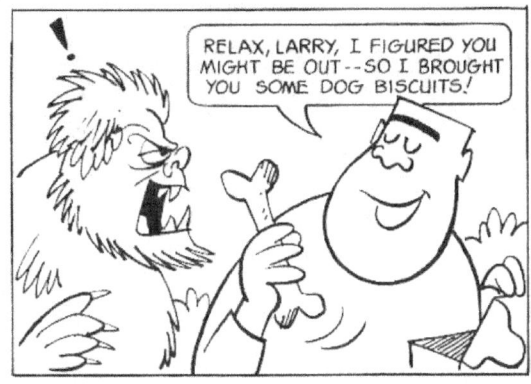

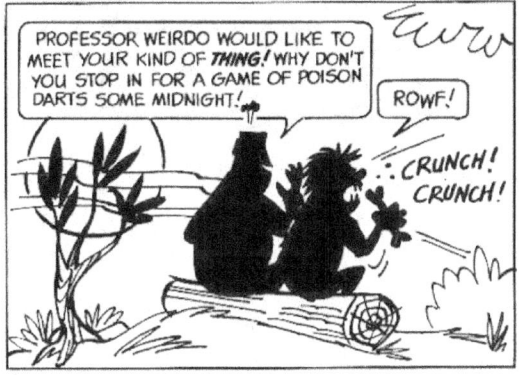

Story panels from Gold Key's "Milton the Monster and Fearless Fly" #1 comic book. *Copyright 1965 Hal Seeger Productions.*

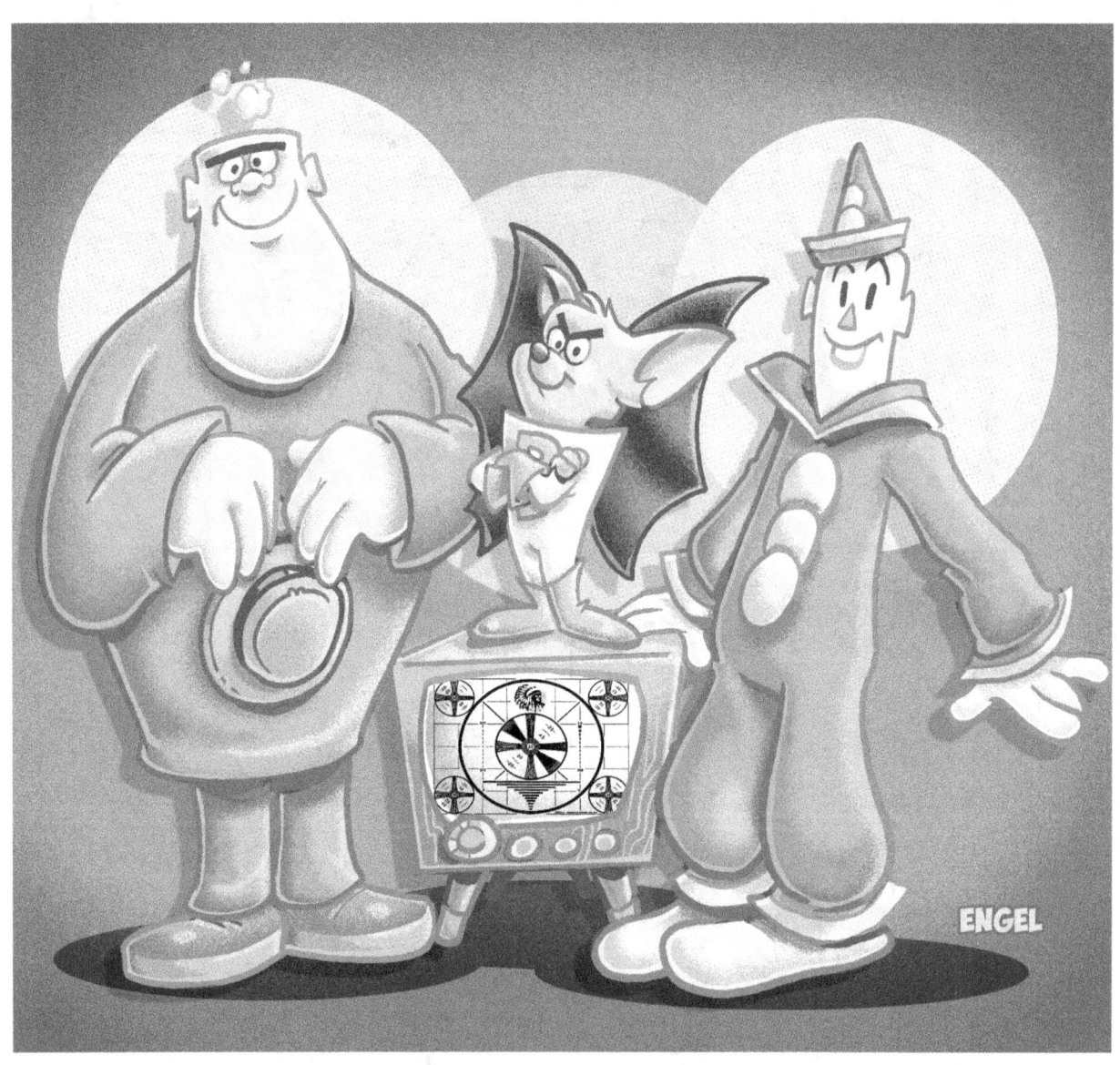

Hal Seeger 1917-2005

Milton the Monster, Batfink and Koko the Clown, illustration by Jim Engel.
Copyright Hal Seeger Productions, Fleischer Studios.